KW-054-491

Air and Water Activities

Dorothy Diamond

Hulton Educational

LIVERPOOL INSTITUTE
OF HIGHER EDUCATION

Order No./Invoice No.
L2364/147829/£8.02

Accession No.
171703

Class No.
372.5T DIA

Control No.
ISBN

Catal.
12/5/94

First published in Great Britain 1984 *by*
Hulton Educational Publications Ltd
Raans Road, Amersham, Bucks HP6 6JJ

Text © Dorothy Diamond 1984
Illustrations © Hulton Educational 1984

All rights reserved. No part of this publication may
be reproduced, stored in a retrieval system, or
transmitted in any form or by any means,
electronic, mechanical, photocopying, recording or
otherwise, without the prior written consent of
Hulton Educational Publications Ltd.

ISBN 0 7175 1187 1

Artwork by John Hopkins
Cover by Julia Osorno
Edited and designed by Ela Ginalska
Photographs by Bob Bray

Phototypeset by Input Typesetting Ltd, London
Printed in Great Britain by
The Pitman Press, Bath

Contents

Introduction

To everybody who likes doing experiments

Air and water are free, clean, harmless and interesting. Do as many of these experiments as you can, and think about what is happening while you are doing them. Make notes and diagrams as scientists do. You can invent more ways of testing for yourself, and you can find out a lot of real science from air and water. What you learn will help you to understand much more difficult experiments when you come to them later on. Go ahead, and enjoy 'working like a scientist'.

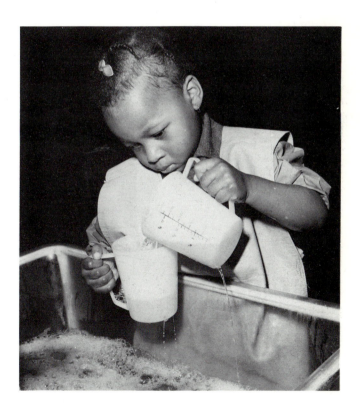

Notes to teachers

About the book

This is a source book of experiments, using very common materials to show very important scientific facts and principles. The results of the experiments form a sound basis for much more advanced science, and the simple treatment makes it possible for quite young children to understand as well as to observe what happens. Almost all of the activities can be carried out by individual children or by pairs or very small groups. Nobody gets bored and everybody can have their turn to do something practical.

The text is arranged in direct form, addressed to pupils. This is to make it easier for teachers either to read it with the children or to hand copies of the book over to the more able readers so that they can go ahead on their own.

The general principle is that in each topic there should be a number of child-sized experiences, so that from their discoveries the pupils can build up their own generalizations. After two or three 'parallel' experiences the 'ah-ha!' effect may well occur—'ah-ha, *now* I see what happens' and perhaps even *why* it happens. This is invaluable for genuine comprehension of later stages in science. Some open-ended questions are included, and logical thinking is encouraged, but the text and the experimental results supply the backing.

The book contains enough materials for a year's work with a class, or it can be used throughout a four- or five-year programme. Groups of experiences will fit very well into topic work, and many experiments would be very effective for assemblies or Open Day displays—popular both with the visitors and with the pupils who explain the exhibits.

The experiments in this book illustrate some of the main ideas which pupils can gain from work with air and water. There are many, many more!

Equipment

Most of the 'apparatus' is familiar everyday material, though a few pieces of standard equipment need to be bought if the school does not already have them. Some pieces will already be in stock in the mathematics department and they can all be regarded as an investment—since, although rather expensive at first, they are also durable.

Skills and methods

The teacher's part in 'doing science' with primary pupils is quite different from the old idea of 'teaching' science—which meant telling them 'facts' and getting children somehow or other to learn them. The primary teacher today experiences activities with the children—often learning with them in the process. Even the youngest are far more capable than they are often given credit for, if they have the concrete 'things' in their hands, and much discovery can take place without much vocabulary. To give an example from a multi-lingual nursery-infant classroom, a tiny Asian girl, just 4½, discovered the displacement of water—like old Archimedes—by immersing first her fingers, then hand, then forearm, in a measuring jar of water, without any kind of stimulus from the teacher, and without a word spoken on either side. She clearly knew what happened, checked her result, and extended the experiment of her own accord—following the rise and fall of the water in the jar with a finger of the other hand. The teacher learnt at the same time.

Teachers usually have to plan the broad outlines of experimental work, simply because the apparatus has to be available and the kind of activity has to be suitable; the teacher does not have to know a lot of scientific facts. Facts are not the main aim of primary science; skills, attitudes and methods of working are the most important factors, which accounts for the general lack of 'primary science syllabuses'. Of course, some materials are better than others for practice of such skills and methods. Water is one of the very best—for physical skills, for accurate observation, for reasoning and for habits of scientific method such as predicting (making a sensible guess), testing the prediction, repeating 'to make sure' and checking that the test is a 'fair' test.

The teacher will decide how much recording the pupils will do, and in what form. It is strongly recommended that some kind of record is made; if children are not expected to keep any record of their experiments and discoveries, they may well get the feeling that these are not considered to be worth recording. Adult scientists regularly make diagrams, sketches and notes of their work, so it is good training. Discussion and other ways of communicating ideas and results are also essential—both to adult and child scientists.

Working with air and water

Air and water, the materials of the activities in this book, are so essentially part of our lives and our life that there are hundreds of everyday topics connected with them. Every discovery children make about air and water helps them to understand their, and our, world.

Teachers sometimes avoid work with water because of the spills, overflows and 'mess'. Part of the problem may be that the children have been used to 'playing about' in the big water-tray—this is valuable in its own way, but the tray tends to become too full of objects, which leads to lack of space and a tendency towards 'splashing' games. For the 'play', which can be highly scientific—and all teachers know the difference between the two activities—smaller containers are far more satisfac-tory. The plastic boxes (in which delicatessen coun-ters have coleslaw or soft white cheese), somewhat flatter than a cube in shape, are excellent. Each child can have one, or two can share; everything that happens is clearly visible, and clearing up is easy. Splashes and spills are probably best dealt with by having plenty of newspaper handy, both as 'tablecloth' and to flop on top of water which gets on the floor. Children can then forget about it, and just roll up the damp paper at the end of the day.

Another general problem with water experiments is that, especially in some kinds of not quite clear plastic, it is difficult for children to see how high up the water comes. A very few drops of food colouring, as sold for colouring cake icing, solves this problem. The colouring is harmless, but may stain clothes, so care is needed. If the children fill a plastic jug with water and add the colour them-selves, they know that it is coloured water; if the teacher gets it ready in advance, how are they to know that it is not paraffin or pink gin?

Air presents much greater problems of identifica-tion. Invisible, and too light for simple classroom weighing, it is best detected by 'feel', as in a blown-up plastic bag or balloon, or by feeling a current of moving air. Children do not easily grasp the fact that an 'empty' clear beaker upside down and pressed into water is not filled with water because of the air in it. The linking experience may well be obser-vation of bubbles coming out of 'empty' things when under water. Blowing bubbles in water for comparison may help—but we have to remember the small boy who objected 'That's not air, Miss, that's me bref!'—something much more personal.

Concepts

The notes on the sections, at the back of this book, suggest the concepts which can spring from the activities. They also correct here and there old or incorrect statements which are still too frequent in printed books and schemes.

L. I. H. E.
THE MARKLAND LIBRARY
STAND PARK RD., LIVERPOOL, L16 9JD

Light and heavy things; floating or sinking

1. As light as air

People say something is 'as light as air'. Is air so light? Try some tests to see how light air really is.

1. Put some water in a wide, quite deep tray or something like a fish-tank without any fish. Now blow up a balloon—it doesn't matter how full, so long as you don't burst it. Fasten the neck securely (you can fold it back and put a rubber band tightly round it, or you can tie it in a knot—if you can pull the neck long enough to tie). Then drop the balloon on the water, and look as closely as you can to see how far the balloon has sunk into the water. You know from other things that the heavy ones go a long way into the water—they may even go to the bottom. What does the balloon full of air do?

2. And now get some bubble-mixture, either the kind you buy or the kind you make from washing-up liquid in water. With the tube from an old ball-point pen (the outer case) blow some bubbles on top of your bubble-mixture. Then get some bubbles on top of the water in the tray or fish-tank. You can scoop them, or blow them over it and let them drop off on to the water. Look sideways at the top of the water, and see how far the bubbles full of air go into the water. Do they sink at all? This tells you how light air is!

2. Plastic bag boat

Many small boats these days are made of plastic or rubber. They can be rolled up and carried in a car or on a bigger boat, because they are just pumped up with air (inflated) when they are needed. They are often called 'inflatables'. The two sides are usually like two sausages filled with air when they are pumped up.

Try this: get a small plastic bag, blow it up until it is about half full of air, and close it tightly with the usual kind of wire closure. Then flatten the middle of the bag, put it on some water in a water tray or a big bowl, and carefully load your boat with cargo in the middle. You could use plastic cubes or beans or cotton-reels: choose things which will not be spoilt if they get wet.

Is your plastic bag boat too fat? Let a little air out, and close it again. Would it carry more cargo if you blew a little more air into it? Try this. Does it sink slowly? Find out why: you may not have closed it tightly enough, or there may be a hole in the bag. If the bag leaks, get a new one. Have a competition with a friend to see who can make the same-sized plastic boat carry the bigger load.

3. Very light stuff

When you are trying things to see if they float or sink, you find some which float almost on top of the water—they hardly go in at all. Make a collection of different kinds of very light stuff. Pick out things such as cotton-wool and a plastic sponge. Now put each one in a small plastic bag, squeeze the bag until it just fits the stuff inside, and twist the closure wire round the neck. You may be able to get some bits of the quilted material anoraks are made of, an airmail padded bag, a piece of balsa wood, and you can certainly find sheets and lumps of expanded polystyrene.

Try two tests with each kind of very light stuff:
(**a**) feel how light it is on your hand, and then see how high it floats in water;
(**b**) push it under water, and feel as well as see

how it comes up again. Some will always bob up like corks, but some will get wet. What happens when the light stuff gets wet through?

Think about ways in which these kinds of stuff might be used—say for life-jackets, or life-rafts. Some of the stuff might even be dangerous if it got wet . . .

4. Light and heavy

Here is a good piece of science which also makes a good display and talking point—for a class, the school, or a parents' evening.

You need two fairly large water-tanks—fish-tanks without fish, or big washing-up bowls—as alike as possible, and both half-full of water. Then you get together as many pairs of similar things as you can, but in each pair one heavy and one light. Good ideas are a plastic teaspoon and a steel one; a pottery beaker and an expanded polystyrene one; a wooden ruler and a steel one the same size; a large glass marble and a plastic ball the same size and colours; for fun, a rectangular piece of snackbar fruit-cake and an equal-sized piece of spongecake. Think of and look out for other pairs. Then have them all in front of the water-tanks, and let people try guessing and testing—each person choosing a 'pair' to test in water.

Afterwards, think of reasons for having the light ones (plastic knives and forks on aeroplanes?) and the heavy ones (snackbar fruitcake if you're hungry!).

5. Heavy stuff

You know that some things are made of such heavy stuff that they will always sink to the bottom in water. If you go to the seaside, you know that pebbles and rocks won't come floating up the beach, bobbing about on the waves, though other things will do.

Make a collection of the heaviest kinds of stuff you can get hold of—a few stones, some sand tightly done up in a plastic bag, a glass marble or two, a bit of lead (a fishing weight/sinker perhaps, or one of the weights they use to make a car wheel balance) and a few nuts, nails, bolts and screws. Test each one in water, but dry it afterwards if it is stuff which goes rusty.

Put this collection beside your 'very light stuff' display. Then add some things for other people to guess about—a golfball? a knife, fork and spoon? (they ought to know these if they do any washing-up), a piece of wood, and another piece of wood with some nails knocked into it. This will be a real puzzle—you can make it float *or* sink by putting in a few nails or a lot of nails—but let the others guess first and then find out. Don't tell them.

6. Fruit in the water

There is a messy game called 'Bob apple' which people sometimes play at Hallowe'en parties: you put some apples in a bowl of water on a chair (or on the floor) and the players hold their hands behind their backs and try to grab an apple with their teeth. You are clever or lucky if you can get an apple this way. But it tells you something about apples in water—do they sink or float? What is there in the middle of an apple which might help? Think.

Now try several kinds of fruit in water, to see if they float or sink. You can borrow a banana, an orange, a tomato, even a grape or a peach. Putting them in water won't hurt the fruit. Guess for each fruit whether you think it will sink or float, before you try it. Some trees grow beside rivers or ponds; it might make a difference to the seeds of these trees if the fruit floats away or goes to the bottom.

7. Big and little candles

For this you need a tiny birthday-cake candle, an ordinary plain candle or nightlight, and the fattest, chunkiest candle you can find. It does not matter if they are partly burnt away, and they will not be spoilt afterwards. Get some water in a bowl, and then guess—will the tiny candle float or sink? Try it. You were right, weren't you? What about the 'kitchen' candle? Guess, then test. Now for the big chunky Christmas candle—guess again before you put it into the water. Were you right again? Try this on other people too. It tells you something about candle-wax.

8. Two drinks cans

For this you need a new drinks can—not opened— and an 'empty' can of the same sort. You can drink what's in the new can afterwards. Hold one can on each hand, and see how heavy or light they feel. You know exactly which is which without looking.

Now put both cans gently into water in a bowl. You could guess what would happen. Next, push the 'empty' can just a little way into the water. What comes out? What goes in? Push it a little further in—and go on doing this until nothing more happens. Where are the two cans now? Turn the open can the right way up, keeping it under water, and lift both cans out. Hold one can in each hand, the right way up. How do they feel for weight? Why did they feel so different at the beginning?

You sometimes see a drinks can floating in a pond, or in the sea. Can you get your open can to float half in the water and half out? Try it. What will you need to do?

9. What's in an 'empty' drinks can?

All you need for this is an empty drinks can and a bowl of water. Turn the can upside down—is it empty? At least there isn't any more to drink in it. Now push it, still upside down, into the water. Do you have to push? Hold it down, and very carefully tip the can a little bit sideways. What happens? Tilt it a bit more and then a bit more still. Go on tipping it until the can is the right way up. What happened while you were tipping it up? What happens now if you let go of the can? What's in it now? What got out? What was there in the 'empty' can?

10. What's in a funnel?

Find a good big plastic funnel. Look through it—first one way, and then the other. Can you see anything inside the funnel? Of course not; you knew there wasn't anything to see. But does that mean that there isn't anything in the funnel? Try this: you can use the big water-tray if your school has one, or you can put enough water in a bucket for the whole funnel to go in under water. Turn the funnel upside down, put your finger over the hole at the tip of the tube, and push the funnel down to the bottom of the water with the other hand. Then take your finger off—what happens?

Do it again, with a beaker upside down and full of water waiting to catch what comes out of the funnel. There really was something in the funnel, wasn't there?

11. Plasticine or Blu-Tack boats

This makes a good competition, and you find out a lot of science while you are doing it. You each need a small handful of Plasticine or a knob of Blu-Tack about the size of two corks. Blu-Tack is

8

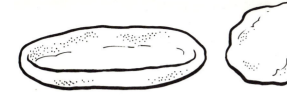

easier to work with, as it will stick even if it is cold and/or wet. Then you need a bowl of water (warm if you are using Plasticine) and newspaper to stand it on.

Put your lump of Blu-Tack or Plasticine into the water gently. You knew what would happen—it would sink. Now take it out, dab it dry, and try to make a boat out of it. This has to float! A flat-bottomed shape, like a raft with turned-up edges, is the best—but you and your friends may have to try several models before it works. It can be done, so go on trying.

Can you do the whole thing all over again—lump, boat, lump, boat . . .? Then you *know* you know how! Remember that the biggest ships are made of steel, but steel is much heavier than Blu-Tack for the same-sized lump.

12. Balancing the boat

Everybody knows that you have to be careful when you get into a small boat: you mustn't put too much weight on one side, or the boat will tip over. Try these two tests:

Get a small, very light tray—the kind that comes from the supermarket with a small piece of meat on it, or a margarine tub. Also get the bottom half of a plastic eggbox (6 eggs) and six glass marbles all alike (in size—the colour doesn't matter). First float the plastic tray or tub. It will float quite flat, and right on top of the water. Now try loading it with marbles. Put one marble in the tray, then try again with two, and again with three, until you have tried with all six marbles. Why did you have to start all over again each time? This wouldn't be very good for a boat and a cargo, would it?

Now float the half-eggbox by itself. Put one marble in one of the egg spaces, then another, then a third, and so on. Why does this work better than with the tray? Try to think out and then test all the possible ways to float the eggbox *level*, using two marbles only. Then make it float level with four marbles (can you find more than one way?)—and finish up with all six marbles on board. These experiments tell you something about loading real boats, with cargo or with people!

13. Deep water or shallow water?

Do things float better, or higher, in deep water or in shallow water? People often tell you that one of these is better for floating ships. Try to find out: get a clear plastic lunch-box or an ice-cream carton, and a deep bucket. Put water in both of them. Instead, you could use water in the sides (shallow) and the middle (deep) of a school water tray if nobody else is using it.

Find three things to test with—all something like a boat. Can you load one of them, perhaps a plastic eggbox, until it is almost sinking but not quite? Can you get something on which you can put a mark to show where the water comes to? Then try your floating things, one at a time, in shallow water and then in deep water. Put each in very carefully, and try to see exactly how high each floats in shallow and in deep water. Try it again with a friend if you are not sure. What did you *think* would happen? Were you right? Does the water down at the bottom really make any difference to what happens at the top?

14. Boat and cargo problem

For this problem you need a 'boat' of some kind—the bottom half of a plastic eggbox will do nicely, a good big lump of Plasticine, and a clear plastic lunch-box or an unused fish-tank. Put the 'boat' on water in the 'lake', and check that it can float with the cargo of Plasticine on board. If not, make the lump of Plasticine smaller—but you need as much as the eggbox can carry.

Now think: what will happen to the level of the top of the water in your lake (1) when you float the boat without any load? (2) when you put the cargo on the boat? (3) if you tip the cargo overboard so that it sinks to the bottom of the lake?

Mark the water level first without anything in the water. You can use wax crayon if the lunch-box or fish tank is dry. If not, use a sticky label on the side, and mark on that. Then make a guess about point (1), and try it to see if you were right. Do the same for point (2), with the Plasticine cargo on board. The last one (3) is the tricky one—what happens to the water level when the cargo goes to the bottom of the 'lake'?

There is another thing to try—what happens to the water level if water gets into the boat? Guess first, and then find out.

15. Lifting sunken things with air

Get an 'empty' drinks can and sink it in water in a bowl or clear container like a small fish-tank. Make it sink and stay at the bottom. You see something coming out of the can while you are doing this. Now take a straw (or a piece of plastic tubing) and poke the end into the hole where the ring-pull came from. Blow gently into the straw, and watch the can. You may be able to get the can floating quite high in the water this way.

Next try raising a model ship with air. Make a ship with Plasticine—any kind of flat boat will do. Sink it, or let it sink itself. To raise the wreck, you need a plastic bag (about 25×38cm off a roll works well), a tube (such as the case from a ball-point pen) and a short piece of elastic to tie round the neck of the bag and keep it tightly on the tube. Slide the bag under the model wreck, and blow gently through the tube. You may have to try more than once—this happens in real life too—but if you can get the middle of the bag under the boat, it will probably work the second time, if not the first.

16. Weight in water?

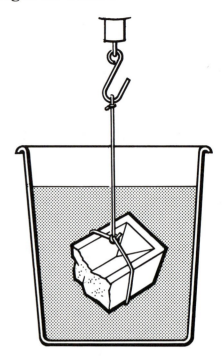

This experiment is about a very important piece of science, so you should do it several times if you can. It is about *weight*, and that means you use a *spring scale* (or spring balance) to measure how much the force of gravity is pulling downwards the thing you are weighing. Now you need something solid and fairly heavy, like a stone or a half-brick—the important thing is to make sure that it is not too heavy for the scale to measure its weight.

Tie a string safely round the object, or put it in a 'net' made from old tights nylon, and hook it on the spring scale. What is its weight? Put this down in your notebook or file. Next comes the special bit: you get a bucket of water, and hang the stone or half-brick in the water, still on the scale, and *not touching the bottom* (or side). What does the spring scale say it weighs now? Write this down too. Is it the same as the weight you found the first time? What do you think could possibly be 'helping to hold the stone or half-brick up'?

Next time you are in the bath, get down with as much of you under water as you can and just see if you can possibly hold yourself up off the bottom with one or two fingers! Can you? Think—could you do that in air, say in the bath when the water has all run out? What sort of difference does the water seem to make?

17. What do floating things seem to weigh?

This works well with a playground football, in its net or in a special 'net' made from old tights nylon. Get a spring balance, better called a spring scale. This is what we use to find *weight*, which is the measure of how much gravity pulls on the thing we are weighing.

Hang your football, in its net, on the spring scale. What does it weigh? Write down the weight. Of course, the spring scale started from 0, zero, didn't it? You checked, didn't you; some springs get stretched, if people have put *very* heavy things on the end, and then they don't start from 0.

Now get something the football can float in—it could be a big bowl, or a bucket, or a dustbin lid upside down, resting on bricks and full of water. Gently let the football, still in its net and still hooked on to the spring scale, down on to the water until it floats. Make sure nothing is pulling anywhere, the ball is floating easily and not held up by the net. What does the spring scale tell you the ball weighs? Write down this result in your notes—it is a very important result. Is it what you thought it would be? The force of gravity is still pulling down on the ball, just as hard as it was before, but something is pushing the ball up at the same time.

18. Anchors and buoys

What is an anchor for? To hold a boat in one place when it is too far to tie it up to something on shore. So what do you need for an anchor? Mainly something heavy enough to stay still at the bottom of the water even when the boat is pulling on the rope (or chain). The special anchor shape is so that it catches if it gets dragged along.

Make a little model boat, and tie it to something you have chosen as an anchor. You will have to leave enough thread to let your boat float. Get it floating in a clear bowl or fish-tank. Now 'make the tide rise' by pouring in more water. Was the thread (cable) long enough? What happened to your boat as the 'tide' rose?

Buoys (get the spelling right!) must stay floating in one place, perhaps to mark a sunken wreck. You could make a good model with a table-tennis ball, thread, and a piece of metal—say an old screw, or a fishing weight—at the bottom of the tank. How will you fix the thread to the ball? Plasticine does

11

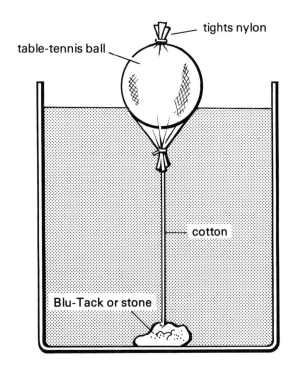

tights nylon

table-tennis ball

cotton

Blu-Tack or stone

not stick well; try Blu-Tack. Or tie the ball up in a small piece of tights nylon! Sea-fishermen's floats are often held in netting. Make a 'sea model'— perhaps with plastic seaweed and a wreck.

19. Does an egg float or sink?

We know the answer, of course, from boiling eggs in a saucepan. You will need a hard-boiled egg for this new test anyway, so check the first part while it cooks. Why do you need the egg hard-boiled? This does not make any difference to the science, but somebody might drop it. . .

While the egg is cooling, get two clear beakers, or glasses half full of cold water. Put into one of them a good big spoonful of salt, and stir and stir. If all the salt disappears, put in some more and stir again. Make the water as salty as you can.

Now use the spoon to lower the egg gently into

the other beaker, into the plain water. Does it float or sink? You knew what would happen. You can guess what might happen next, when you take the egg out of plain water and let it down into the strong salt water. What does happen?

If you have two hard-boiled eggs, as alike as possible, you could put them into the two beakers side by side—and ask somebody (who doesn't know what you did first) to guess how you made it work.

20. The doubtful egg

For this you need a hard-boiled egg, half a beaker of plain water, and half a beaker of the strongest salt water you can make (by stirring salt into it till there is a little left at the bottom). If you have a funnel which will reach right to the bottom of your beaker, it makes the next part a bit easier.

If you have the right funnel, stand it up in the beaker half full of plain water, and carefully pour the strong salt water down it to the bottom of the plain water. If you haven't got a funnel, float a small piece of paper on the strong salt water, and very gently pour the plain water on to the paper. Either way, you want to finish up with the bottom half of the beaker full of salt water, and the top half full of plain ('fresh') water. Take out the paper. Now (of course, gently) let the egg go into the top of the water. You knew by this time what to expect—but it will surprise other people.

21. Straws and rafts

Collect between 10 and 20 ordinary straws. They need not be new ones—if they have been used, just rinse them under the tap. Cut them in half with scissors and leave them to drain while you fill a bowl with water. Take one half-straw, and drop it into the water *upright*. It may sink, or it may float—this depends on what it is made of.

Now take at least six of your half-length straws, and lay them on the top of the water, side by side. What do they do? What do you think is inside these half-straws? Can you find out if your guess is right? Put them back on top of the water, and lay the same number of straws on top of the first lot, but across them—at right angles. Can you make a raft with them? Perhaps you can weave a piece of cotton up and down between some more of the short straws, to hold them together into a flat raft. Load the raft with some fairly light cargo, say Unifix cubes. Find out how to spread them out so that the raft does not tip up.

Have a competition to see how many Unifix cubes you can load on a raft made of 20 half-length straws. What made the straws float so well?

22. A float to measure with

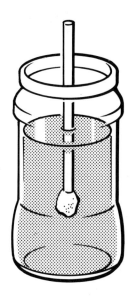

There is a special scientific kind of float called a *hydrometer* (hy-drom-eter), which is used in big dairies, in garages, and in very big breweries! It is put into the milk, to see if anyone might have mixed in some water. It is put into the acid in the car battery to see if the battery is run down. It is floated in the beer to see how strong the beer is!

Quite an important thing, a hydrometer. And a simple one is very easy to make. Find a straw: a milk straw will do, or a milk-shake straw is even better. Get some Blu-Tack—about as big a lump as the small size of marble. Make a round knob of this, and just push it gently on to one end of the straw, blocking up the hole. If you are using a wide straw the marble size is right; if it's a milk or lemonade straw, use half the marble-sized piece.

Then let your hydrometer down, Blu-Tack end first, into water in a tall glass jar. A big instant-coffee jar would be just right. Get the straw floating straight up, then find some way to mark on the straw the place where the water comes up to. A 'marker' felt-tip pen is good for this, because it is waterproof. Test your mark again. Now make some strong salt water in the same jar, and float your hydrometer in this. You see how it works!

Displacement of air and water

23. What makes cotton wool so light?

That's easy, isn't it? You make your guess—and then, being scientific, you test it. Try it this way: get a small pot with a lid (say a small peanut-butter pot, or a sample cream jar). Fill it with cotton wool and screw the top on. Next, find a plastic funnel and an empty fish-tank (or a deep bowl, but the fish-tank is better). Fill the tank with water (not *too* full), and sink a clear beaker in it.

Now you will need a partner to help: put the cotton wool-filled jar in the water, hold the funnel upside down over it, and hold the beaker upside down and full of water over the funnel. If one of

e funnel and the beaker, the other one
lid off the cotton wool-filled jar still
m of the tank.
you can *see* what made the cotton wool
d you can measure how much of it there
was in the cotton wool.

24. A beaker full of marbles

Collect (or borrow) enough small marbles to fill a
clear beaker—plastic or glass, so long as you can
see through it. Put marbles into the beaker with a
gentle shake now and again, so that it is just full
to the top edge. Right—the beaker is full of marbles,
but is it really *full*? Pour some water into the beaker
on top of the marbles, and watch where it goes.
Go on pouring until the beaker is *really* full.

What was in the spaces between the marbles
before you put the water in? Can you find out how
much water you put in? There are different ways
of doing this—you could pour the water out into
a measuring jar, holding the marbles back, or you
could start again from the beginning and see how
much water goes in from a measuring jar or jug.

25. Rolling marbles into water

To start with, you need two clear plastic beakers or
tumblers (alike), a funnel and a measuring jar or
jug. Colour some water, and fill one beaker exactly
to the top with it, not spilling any. Carefully tip
this water through the funnel into the measuring
jar to find out how much water filled the beaker.

Now stand the beaker in a large margarine tub
or ice-cream container, and fill it right to the top
again. Get some small glass marbles, and slide one
at a time into the water. You know what will
happen, of course. Go on until the marbles are just
level with the top of the beaker. Then lift it out
carefully. How much water has overflowed? Pour
this water from the container into the spare
beaker. Did you think it would be half full, or less
than half full, or more?

Measure this water which overflowed, using the
measuring jar. Compare it with the beaker-full you
measured at the beginning. How much water did the
marbles push out? This is the water they *displaced*.

26. Green man goes down

Get some Blu-Tack or green Plasticine, and make
a chunky little blue or green man. Now find a clear
jar or beaker big enough for him to go right to the
bottom. Put enough water into it so that he will
go right under. Now tie a thread round his neck,
and let him down into the water quite slowly. Pull
him up again—what happened to the top level of
the water? Do it again, watching carefully.

Next, mark the top of the water—the water level.
You can use a marker pen on the jar, or a rubber
band round the jar, or a sticky label. See where the
water comes up to when the little green man is
right out of the jar, and when he is right at the
bottom of the water. Let him in slowly, and watch
the level change as he goes in. Pull him out, and
watch the level as he comes out again.

This is a very important experiment because of
what you see and what you find out.

Measuring and weighing water

27. How big is a litre?

One litre is the measure for orange squash and lemonade. The big drinks bottles hold 1½ or even 2 litres. So we need to know what *a litre* looks like.

Collect some plastic bottles, some big ones and some smaller ones. Find some clear beakers if you can—a kind called 'Glacier' are good. Your school may have a clear plastic cube measuring 10 centimetres each side, and perhaps some strong clear plastic bowls and pots. Then if possible get hold of a tall plastic measuring jar with markings down the side; the kind you need has 1000 ml (one thousand millilitres) near the top. One thousand milli*litres* (not milli*metres*—be careful) is **one litre**.

Fill this jar up to the top mark with water you have coloured with some food colouring. Pour this **litre** of coloured water into one of the big bottles. Then fill up your measuring jar again, and pour the second **litre** into another jar or bottle or dish. Put out a row of clear beakers, and pour the next **litre** of coloured water into as many of these beakers as you need to hold it all. Stand all your bottles and jars and beakers on a table, so that people can see just what **one litre** looks like. It makes a good show; it looks even better if you can use different colours, but each lot of water is **one litre**.

28. A cube as big as a litre

This sounds a little odd, but you can easily make a cube box which will hold a litre. The only thing you need to know is that 1 millilitre is the same volume as 1 cubic centimetre. You know cubic centimetres very well; some centimetre cubes are called Centicubes (plastic ones), and there are wooden ones in mathematics apparatus. Just check

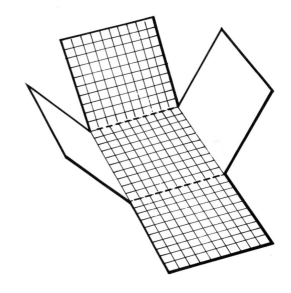

some of them—they measure 1 centimetre each way. Now, if each of these has the same volume as 1 millilitre, 1000 of them will have the same volume as 1000 millilitres, and that is 1 litre.

The best way to make your paper box is to get centimetre-squared paper and draw out the 10-centimetre squares you need for the sides. This will need a bit of thinking, because ordinary paper is only 21 cm wide, and not quite 30 cm high. Stick the pieces together with sticky tape.

Now fill the box (it does not need a lid) with 1 litre of sawdust, or small beads, or birdseed, or lentils, or whatever you can find which is not too heavy and will fit neatly into the corners. Now check, by pouring the boxful into a 1-litre measuring jar or jug. Does it go in? Does it fill the jar or jug (more or less) to the 1 litre (1000 ml) mark?

If you have a plastic cube the same size as your paper one, try the same test with water!

29. Measuring water

Collect all the measuring jugs, jars and beakers you can find. Look carefully at the markings on them, and put them in a row with the one which will hold most on the left, and the one which will hold least on the right. The top marking on each of these tells you its *capacity*—that is how much it can hold. Of course, the top mark isn't right up to the very top edge—you can see why not.

Now fill each of your jugs, jars and beakers exactly to its top mark. This tells you the *volume* of the water in each one.

The marks will probably be like this: 100 ml or 500 ml or 1000 ml, or even for a big one 2000ml. You know that the ml is short for milli*litres*, and that one thousand of these millilitres is *one litre*.

Get one of those big, clear plastic lemonade bottles. Guess its capacity, and then use one of your marked jugs or jars or beakers to see how much water it will hold. (A funnel will help to get the water in quickly and without spilling it.)

30. How big is a drop?

People sometimes say 'put in a drop of this', and on medicine bottles it sometimes says 'take five drops in water'. But how big is a drop, and can drops be bigger or smaller? Think of ways to find out. Here are some ideas to start with.

1. A drop of water will spread out as far as it can in a coloured tissue, a toilet tissue, or in coloured blotting paper. Try to make different-sized drops on, say, a piece of blue or pink toilet paper. Wait a little, till the drop doesn't spread any more—then you can even measure across it, if it is more or less round. Try the next—a bigger one? And the next—a tiny drop.

2. If you can get a dropper, the kind people use to drop 'medicines' into their eyes, nose or ears, wash it out very carefully. Then make a mark on the tube with a wax crayon, and fill it up exactly to this mark. You can see how to go on from here.

After you have tried plain water several times—a scientist always does this kind of experiment more than once to make sure—use water with a little washing-up liquid in it. Are the drops the same size this time?

Think of other ways to find out how big drops are—what about counting how many drops it takes to fill a bottle cap? And so on. . .

31. Finding the weight of some water

Gravity pulls things down; this is what gives them their weight. Gravity on the moon is only one-sixth as strong as it is here on the earth, so things only weigh a sixth on the moon of what they would weigh here.

The best way to see how gravity works is to see how much it stretches a spring. You need a spring 'balance' (better name— spring scale), a place to hang it up so that it is not touching anything, a small plastic bag without holes, a wire closure, and some water.

Make a small hole through the back and front of the plastic bag near the top, to hang it on the hook of the spring scale. Now put some water in the bag—perhaps so that it is about half full, twist the closure tightly round the neck of the bag, and hook it on the spring scale. Look at the scale and see what the pointer points to; this is the *weight* of the water (and of the plastic bag—which is so small that it will hardly show by itself. Try it.) Gravity pulls the water down, and this stretches the spring.

Do the experiment with other things, and with other quantities of water. Find their weights.

32. Finding the mass of some water

Mass and weight are different, though people often muddle them up. The mass of something is how much of it there is, how much of the stuff it is made of. Think about this—there would be just as much metal in a coin if you took it to the moon, but it would feel very much lighter. Its mass would be the same as on earth, but its weight would only be one-sixth (because weight depends on gravity).

We measure mass by balancing it against things which have a mass we already know; these are the things called 'weights', which is a very silly name for them. A little piece of plastic which is called 'a one-gram weight' ought to be called a one-gram mass.

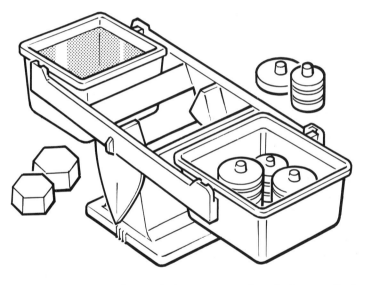

Now, get a beam balance or rocker balance, find as many one-gram masses as you can, and some water. Pour a little water (about a cupful) into one pan of the balance, and balance it exactly with 1-gram masses. What is the mass of water? Empty this water away, and measure some water, say a yogurt-pot full, into the pan. Find its mass. Do this two or three times. Do you always get the same answer? Look at the side of the yogurt pot—it may tell you what the mass of the yogurt was when it was sold!

33. How much does water weigh?

This is a question without an answer, isn't it? Does it mean a drop of water, or the Atlantic Ocean? So let's ask a better question: *what is the mass of 100 millilitres of water*? There are measuring beakers, jugs and measuring jars—all with 100ml marked on them. Find one, and get the water just exactly to the mark. Now check that the rocker-balance balances without anything in either pan. Then pour the 100 ml of water into one pan, and put some of the one-gram plastic things called 'weights' (which ought to be called *masses*) into the other pan, one at a time, until the two sides exactly balance again.

Take the 'weights' out of the pan and count them. You may have had the good idea of counting them as you put them in, but it is always better to check afterwards as well. Now, what number of grams balanced the 100 ml of water you started with? So your experiment says that the mass of 100 millilitres of water is how many grams? This is a very important result, and you should do it very carefully, and several times; perhaps you can get your friends to do it too and see if they get the same result as you do.

34. What is the mass of *one millilitre of water*?

A single millilitre (or cubic centimetre) of water is so small that we cannot get good answers with the usual balances and measuring jars. Try it, and you will see. So what we do is to find the mass of, say, 100 millilitres of water, and divide the answer by 100 to find out the mass of 1 millilitre. Try this, measuring out the 100 ml as carefully as you can, and doing it more than once—to check your result, as scientists do.

When you have done that, you can do something else scientists do—you can make a scientific guess and then test it. Guess what will be the mass of 200 millilitres of water, then test your guess. Then try other measured volumes of water—say 50 or 150 millilitres. The more times you guess and test, the more sure you will be that you know how to get the right answer every time!

And what is the mass of *one* millilitre of water?

35. Weighing water and weighing salty water (finding their masses)

For this experiment you need a pair of plastic scales, or a rocker or beam balance. You will also need a good measuring jar; the tall kind is best.

Now make some really strong salt water. Stir salt into a big mugful of water until there is some salt at the bottom which stays there even when you have stirred and stirred. With the measuring jar,

measure out an exact amount (an exact *volume*) of the salty water. Pour this carefully into one of the plastic 'buckets' (or pans) of the balance. Put enough weights into the other pan (or bucket) to balance the salt water exactly. Count up the weights to see how much the salt water weighed (its mass).

Next wash out the balance pan, putting the salt water back into your mug for other experiments. Measure out exactly the same volume of plain tap-water with the measuring jar, and weigh this just as you did the salt water. Does the plain water weigh exactly the same as the salt water, or more, or less? Think how you made the salty water, and see if you think you have got the right answer.

A real scientist would do this experiment two or three times, just to make sure.

Water pressure

36. Water pressure—water resistance

Have you ever tried to run in the shallow end at the swimming baths? Or to run in the sea when it is up to your knees? You could even try a few steps in the bath, so long as you don't splash too much. Running in water is much harder, and therefore slower, than without the water—isn't it?

Try this experiment: put your hand right inside a small plastic bag without any holes in it. Then push your hand down into water in a bucket, or in the sink. Spread your fingers out, and wave your hand about in the water. Can you feel the pressure of the water against the bag, which pushes the bag against your hand?

Think about the plastic 'fins' which divers wear to help them swim fast under water. They use the flat 'flippers' to push against the water, so it can work both ways. What animals and birds can you think of which have webbed feet for fast swimming? You know from your experiment how it helps them.

37. What difference does the depth make?

The deeper you go in water, the more water there is on top of you—right? But testing this would be a difficult experiment, so try it on a small scale like this:

Get a big plastic bottle—one of the big, clear drinks bottles would be good. Make some small, neat holes in the side—say four, one above the other in a line, at about equal distances apart. A compass point would make all the holes the same size and shape. Now block the holes by sticking a strip of sticky tape right down the side to cover them. Fill the bottle to the neck with water, and stand it on the side of the sink with the holes over the sink. Hold the bottle firmly and quickly strip off the sticky tape. Watch the water coming out of the holes. How did the water come out of the top hole? How did it come out of the bottom hole? Do the experiment again, to see everything that happens.

To test what difference pressure makes to the way water comes out of a small hole, try this (in the playground). Fill a washing-up liquid bottle with water, hold it horizontally, pointing away from you (and from other people) and test what happens with a gentle squeeze, and a hard squeeze. What sort of squirt do you get with a light pressure, and with strong pressure? Think back to the bottle with holes in the side—you can see why different things happened.

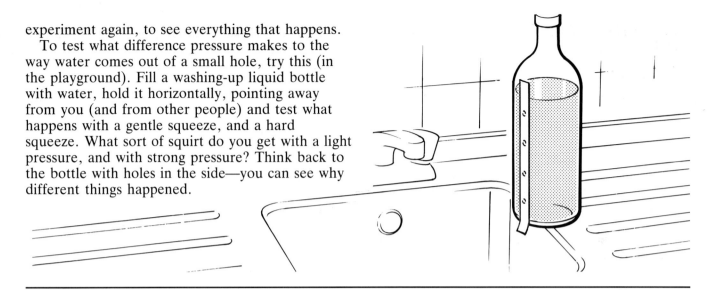

Hot and cold water and air

38. Stir the bathwater!

This is a true story: somebody runs hot and cold water from the two taps into the bath. They dip a toe in—it's hot. The person gets into the bath, and sits down—into cold water. . . (Some baths have mixer taps so that this can't happen.)

Try this experiment—with two jam-jars instead of a bath. Get two jars alike, stand them on newspaper, and fill one to the very top with cold water. Put a few drops of food colouring into the other jar, and fill this one to the very top with hot water. Now slide a piece of stiff card across the top of this jar, hold it carefully, and turn it upside down on top of the cold one. Still holding the top (hot) jar, carefully slide out the card, so that one jar stands on top of the other. Watch the water for a minute or two, then leave it, and look again after about five minutes. Where is the hot water—the coloured water? (Remember the bathwater?) Feel the outside of each jar; can you feel which was which?

Warning: don't have the water too hot for your hands. Just have it 'hot-bath hot'.

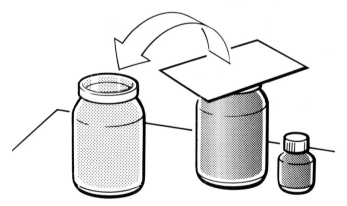

39. Cold water on top of hot water?

Start again with two equal jam-jars. Fill one of them using hot water with food colouring, right to the very top. This one will be the bottom jar this

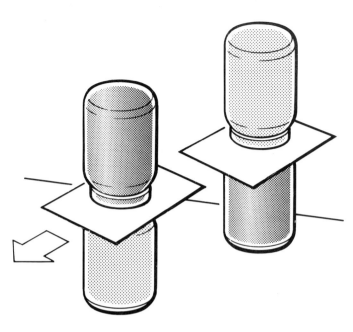

Get the outside tube of a ball-point pen, the clear colourless kind. Block up the little hole in the side (if there is one) with a tiny spot of Blu-Tack. Then make a fat ring of Blu-Tack round the tube, near one end. Fill a clear plastic lemonade bottle with coloured water right to the very top edge, and fix the ball-point tube, short end down, into the neck of the bottle with the Blu-Tack, so that it is water-tight. This is a very simple water thermometer. To see how it works, stand the bottle in a bowl of hot water for some minutes—it does not work very fast, because the water takes time to warm up.

To cool the water down, and make it colder than the room, stand the bottle in a bowl of cold water with some ice cubes in it. If you want to try this again, you may have to take the tube and Blu-Tack out and refill the bottle to the very top again, but this is easy to do.

Real thermometers have mercury or coloured alcohol in them—but the way they work is the same. If you can use a longer tube, say clear plastic, your thermometer will be much better!

41. Feeling cold and wet

Feeling wet and feeling cold often go together, don't they? Think about getting out of the sea or the swimming baths on a chilly day—or standing about in the rain with wet hair and wet trousers or jeans and wet socks.

Do a few tests to find out more about it, but without getting too wet or too cold. Start by using your hands for a test: dip one hand in water, keep the other one dry, hold them in front of you, side by side, and get someone to fan them quite hard with a folded newspaper. Can you feel any differ-ence? Using two hands like this, so that you can compare them, is a bit of good science. What will happen to the wet hand if your partner goes on fanning long enough? The same thing happens to your wet clothes if you go on wearing them long enough too—doesn't it?—and to your wet hair.

time. Fill the other jar with cold water, also to the brim, and slide a piece of stiff card across the top. Hold this firmly, turn the (cold) jar upside down, and put it on top of the hot-water jar. Make a guess about what might happen, if anything. Then slide the card out from between the two jars. Test your guess by watching the coloured hot water in the bottom jar and the plain cold water in the top one.

Look back at the other hot-and-cold-water exper-iment and see which lot of water stayed on top. In the second experiment, the two lots of water started to change places; when this happens it is called a *convection current*.

40. Water thermometer

Water is not good stuff to make thermometers with—for one thing, think what happens to it on a frosty night! But a very simple bottle-and-tube apparatus can show something about thermome-ters and how they work.

On a windy day, get two kitchen paper towels or cloths, one wet and the other dry, and hang or hold them up for a minute or two. Then feel them. Does one feel colder than the other? You could try this test very well with the two ends of a bath-towel, one wet end and one dry end. In fact, you may have tried this without meaning to, if you have let part of the towel dip into the water. And the water will have been warm, but the wet bit will soon feel cold just the same.

42. Does hot air rise?

People often talk about 'hot air rising'. How can you find out if this really happens? We can't see air, so you would have to find some other way to test it.

First, light a short, fat candle or a nightlight so that the flame will give you some hot air. Carefully put your hands round the sides of the flame and move them in until it feels warm. Notice how near this is. Now hold one hand *high up* over the flame. Can you feel the hot air coming up to your hand? Use your common sense. There is no need to burn yourself!

To show that something is happening, try this: cut out a circle of stiff foil—say the bottom of a pie-tray. Cut towards the middle about 8 or 10 times, spacing your cuts evenly, and each time going about three-quarters of the way in. Give each vane a twist, all in the same direction. Spike a

glass-headed pin loosely through the exact centre, and push it into a cork. Hold the cork, and let your foil circle hang over the flame. Move it up and down (but not into the flame!) to find a good place—where something happens. What happens? Why does something happen? (You can even do this test with a foil milk-bottle top, but wash it first.)

43. Can you see hot air?

There is an easy answer to this—you cannot see air anyway, so—no. But there is something rather strange: you can sometimes see '*shadows*' of things you can't see. Try it this way:

Find a place where the sun is shining through the window on to a white wall, or put up a piece of white paper there. Light a short, fat candle or a nightlight, and hold it carefully in the sun between the window and the wall. Look at the wall.

If the sun isn't shining, use the brightest torch in the darkest corner. Or, even better, use the slide projector without a slide. You can stand your candle safely on the table between the projector and the wall. Watch the shadow of the hot air over the flame. What can you see?

44. Puzzle experiment

This test is easy to do, and you can guess what is going to happen—and get it right. But it seems to puzzle quite a few people, even people who write books and put this experiment in them.

You need two 'empty' drinks cans—the best kind are the small 'slim' cans from fruit juices. Pull the ring, drink the juice and then cut the top right out with a tin-opener, leaving a smooth edge. Now you need three more things: a little dish of bubble-mixture (this could be just washing-up liquid and water), a bowl (or saucepan) of hot water, and another of cold water with ice-cubes in it.

Dip the top edges of the two drinks cans in the bubble mixture— this will quite easily give you a flat 'bubble', a flat film, over the top of each. Stand one can in the hot water (you will have to hold it, of course) and the other in the very cold water. What happens to the bubble film on the top of each can? What makes the difference? (There is only one thing which is different for the two cans, isn't there!) If the film lasts long enough you can change the cans over, just to test your scientific guess. If the film breaks, make another one.

45. What does air do when you heat it and cool it?

To find out one of the most important things air does when you heat it and cool it, all you need is a large empty washing-up liquid bottle, an ordinary balloon and two bowls or buckets—one of cold water and one of hot water.

Lever the little cap off the top of the bottle and fit the neck of the balloon on to the neck of the bottle. Then just hold the bottle as far as it will go—perhaps half-way—in the hot water. Watch the balloon. It will show you what the air inside is doing. Then take it out of the hot water and hold it in cold water instead. It is a good idea to change from hot to cold and back again several times; scientists like to check their results by seeing if they will happen more than once.

The result of this 'air' experiment is important because it helps to explain why other hot-air experiments work.

46. A kind of air-thermometer

This is not a thermometer which will tell you how hot it is today, but it will show you something about what happens when air gets warmer or colder. All you need is a clear plastic lemonade bottle, a clear straw or (better) the outside tube from an old ball-point pen, a beaker of coloured water and some Blu-Tack. And a newspaper to stand them on.

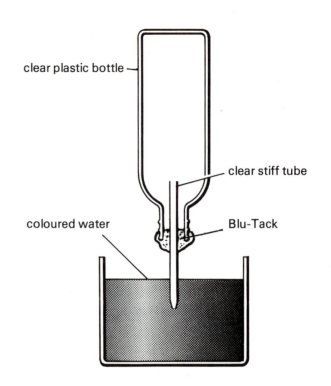

clear plastic bottle

clear stiff tube

coloured water

Blu-Tack

Put a ring of Blu-Tack round the tube, and block up the little hole in the side of the tube if there is one. Fit the Blu-Tack ring into and round the neck of the bottle so that it is airtight, and so that the tube sticks out. Now hold the bottle upside-down by its neck, and dip the tube into coloured water in the beaker. Warm the air in the bottle by putting warm hands round it (but don't squeeze!) What do you see happening in the beaker? What does this tell you about the air you are warming?

If you want to make the air warmer still, wring out a cloth in hot water and wrap this gently round the bottle. Finish this part of your testing by cooling the bottle and the important air inside it by wrapping the bottle (top end only) in a cloth wetted with cold water. Watch at the bottom to see what happens in the pen-tube and the neck of the bottle.

What does the experiment of warming and cooling the air in the bottle tell you?

Water and air pressures

47. A tumbler full of air

Any kind of clear glass or plastic tumbler will do for these three tests, but the tests will look even better if you can use the tumblers in a clear bowl or fish-tank without any fish.

The tests all work in the same way—you push the tumbler upside-down into the water, but with different things inside it.

1. Push a dry paper tissue, coloured if possible, into the tumbler as far as it will go. Make sure it will stay there when you turn the tumbler upside down. Then push the tumbler, open 'top' downwards, into the water. Look carefully at the water inside the tumbler, and at the tissue. Then take the tumbler out again, and see if the tissue is wet. Did you think it would be?

2. Drop a whole peanut shell (and nuts inside it) into the water, and press the tumbler upside down over it, right down to the bottom of the water. What happens to the peanut 'diver'?

3. Do the same thing with a tiny model boat made of expanded polystyrene—from a piece of packing. Look carefully to see just where inside the tumbler the boat is floating.

What do these three little tests say about the air in the tumbler?

48. If the funnel fits the bottle-neck. . .

Collect a funnel and two or three different bottles. Try pouring water into the bottles without using the funnel. Then put the funnel into the neck of one of your bottles (emptied, of course) and see if the funnel makes it easier to fill the bottle. This is what funnels are for, isn't it? But sometimes it doesn't work, and the water stays in the funnel instead of running through.

Try two or three bottle-necks; can you find one which only *just* lets the funnel in—a tight fit? You could make it fit tightly by putting a ring of Blu-Tack round the stem of the funnel and pressing it on to the bottle-neck. What happens now when you pour water into the funnel?

What is there in the bottle before the water goes in? Perhaps if the water goes in, something else has to get out to leave room for it? Try poking a straw down the funnel—could this help?

Plastic funnels often have ridges down the outside of the narrow part (the stem) so that they do not fit tightly into bottles. You can now think why.

49. Sucking milk up a straw

You want to see what's happening, so use a clear plastic straw if you can, or a short piece of clear plastic tube. Suck up some milk. Can you see it coming up the straw? A mirror might help! Stop sucking, and think about what you did to make the milk come up. Did you make room for it in your mouth? Yes? So as milk came into your mouth, some more came up the straw—keeping the straw full. You know what happens when you get to the bottom of the milk—you get a mouthful of air instead, with funny noises.

Now get the straw full of milk again, and quickly pinch the top of the straw with your finger and thumb. Take it out of your mouth, and hold it up (over the bottle or cup, of course). Does the milk fall out? But you aren't sucking any more—so something must be holding the milk up. What is there at the bottom of the straw to hold it up? Nothing but air! But now watch what happens if you stop pinching the top end, and let air get in at the top of the milk too. Air at both ends—the milk falls out. . .just as it does when you pour it from a jug.

Look at other experiments to find out more about the very important science in this one.

50. A 'stop–start' stream of water

For this you need a coffee-tin with an airtight plastic lid (or a treacle-tin with its lid). Make a small hole in the bottom of the tin—a good way is to hammer a small nail through, into the tin. Stick sticky tape over the hole. Now make a hole in the lid as well; if you put the lid down on a bit of scrap wood, you can use the nail again. (On the tin, it does not work well.)

Fill the tin with water, put the lid on, hold it over a bowl, and peel off the sticky tape from the bottom hole. You knew what would happen. But quickly put your finger on the hole in the lid. Lift your finger, put it back. . . Your finger is not really stopping the water from getting out—what is your finger stopping? Fill up the can, and start with your finger on the hole in the lid. Can you make the stream start and stop as you want it to?

People often use the 'two holes' method to get soup or fruit-juice out of a tin. They make a hole on each side of the top of the tin, and as air can get *in* through the top hole, soup (or juice) can get *out* of the lower one.

51. What makes suckers stick?

Well, it certainly is not sucking which makes them stick, because suckers cannot *do* anything! Look for some suckers: on the tips of 'indoor' arrows, inside shop doors (with a notice saying OPEN/CLOSED), in cars or bathrooms to hold things up. . . And there is a big kind of sucker used to unblock the bath or sink drain. Get hold of at least one you can experiment with, but a real sucker, not a stick-on-the-tiles hook.

Put the sucker down gently on a clean, smooth table-top. Pick it up again—it didn't stick, did it? Now make the round 'sucker' part wet all round, and press it down flat on the table. PULL—and

think what can possibly be holding it down. . . There is nothing on top of it but air! And the wetness underneath stops air from getting underneath—it makes it airtight round the edges.

Try pressing your wet 'sucker' on walls, doors, windows, flat tin-lids—on all sorts of flat things. Does it stay pressed on rough things where air can get underneath, or does it only stay pressed on to smooth things where the air can't get under it?

52. A tumbler of water

This is an experiment everybody knows, but there is still something to find out about it. You need a glass tumbler, a piece of card (like a postcard), a bowl (or the sink), and some water.

Fill the tumbler full to the very top with water, and slide the card across the top, keeping it flat. You may find that you are 'slicing' a little water off! Put one hand over the card to hold it on, and carefully turn the tumbler upside down over the bowl (or sink). Hold the tumbler steady, and take your hand away from the card. What is underneath the card now? What is happening?

The 'science magic' kind of book often says that the tumbler must be absolutely full of water. Must it? Try the same test with a little air in the tumbler before you put the card on. You may need a new card, because although it is good if the card is wet, it is not so good if it bends. Try with about half of the beaker full of air. . .you need a steady hand. . .

What do you find out from your *own* experiments? What do you think they tell you?

53. The famous 'chicken fountain'

All you need for this is a clear plastic lemonade bottle, a deep saucer or a 'take-away' tray, water, and (the most difficult) some kind of stand to fix the bottle to. A stool or a small chair standing on the table will do for the stand, with two pieces of string to tie the bottle to a leg. This is for the model.

The main problem to be solved is to give the

chickens, especially small chicks, a steady supply of drinking water without making it so big or so deep that they can get into it. Also if the water tray is wide—like a tiny pond—it will dry up quickly in hot weather.

You probably know already how to set up the model: you fill the bottle right up with water, hold a hand over the top, turn the bottle upside down and put the open neck into the saucer or tray, as near the bottom as you can. Take your hand away quickly, keeping the neck of the bottle almost touching the tray. You would expect some water to run out, wouldn't you? Does it? Then what happens? This is not a new idea to you, is it? 'If air can't get in, water. . . . .'

Now test the 'fountain', as if you were a lot of thirsty chickens all at the same time: scoop some water out of the tray. What happens? Try it again. It isn't a fountain, in spite of its name—but would it help the chickens?

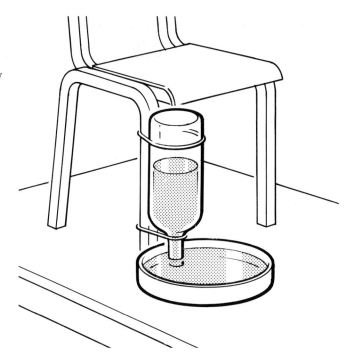

Bounce and bubbles

54. Air and 'bounce'

Blow up a round balloon until it is about half full of air. (Guess this.) Then tie the neck. Blow up another balloon, just the same kind as the first, as far as it will go without risk of bursting. Tie this one too. Now try bouncing both the balloons on the table. Which bounces better? Did you know this would happen?

Feel both balloons with your hands—gently. What can you say about how they feel, and how they bounce? 'The one which bounces better . . .' (you can think of several things to say) 'The balloon which doesn't bounce so well . . .'

Does this tell you anything about bicycle tyres or car tyres?

55. Air and bouncing balls

You need two hollow rubber balls of the same kind, say beach balls or playground footballs. But you need one good one, and one old one with a hole in it.

Try bouncing these two balls in the playground. Throw them hard at the ground, and try to catch them again. What is there inside these two balls? Why does one ball bounce better than the other?

What do you know about bicycle tyres and car tyres which tells you just the same thing?

If you try this test with a split tennis ball, you find that it still bounces a bit. What can still make it bounce at all?

56. Balloon-face

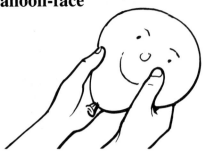

Get a new, round balloon, put it flat on the table, and draw a face on it with a felt-tip pen. Now start to blow up the balloon. Stop once or twice before it is fully blown up, and look at the face. When the ballon is big, but not hard enough to burst, tie the neck. What has happened to the face you drew? Can you make one cheek bulge as if it were eating a big sweet? Can you make the face smaller without letting any air out? If you can, what happens to the rest of the balloon when the face is small?

57. Blowing up balloons—and bicycle tyres

People who want lots of balloons for a party or a dance can use a cheap kind of pump. It is made of two cardboard tubes, one inside the other. Perhaps you can get hold of such a pump. If so, put one finger over the ring into which the neck of the balloon goes, and pump with the other hand. Can you feel the air pushing your finger? Can you feel your other hand pushing the air inside the pump? Does anything happen if you push the pump handle in and then quickly let go?

Work the pump handle several times—in and out—and hold your other hand close to the tip (the nozzle). Now get a balloon, and try blowing it up with the pump. Watch what happens to the balloon each time you push the handle in. Can you blow up a balloon this way as well as you would do with your mouth?

If you have, or can borrow, a bicycle pump, you could try the same things with this kind of pump. It will pump harder than the cardboard one, but it may not be as good for blowing up balloons. Try to think or find out why not.

58. Blowing big bubbles

How can you get the biggest bubbles? Do they come bigger if you blow through a straw? or an old ball-point pen tube? or perhaps through a plastic funnel dipped in the bubble-mixture? Can you make a small bubble bigger if you wet a straw with bubble liquid and poke it into the bubble, blowing into the small one? Some bubble-pots have a plastic ring inside, so that you can blow through it. Does this make a bigger bubble than a straw does? If you pour some bubble liquid (or water with washing-up liquid) into a saucer, the bubbles you make on top of it will probably last longer than the ones you blow in the air—so you have more time to make them bigger, though they are flat underneath.

Can you now blow a lot of very small bubbles on top of the liquid? You can make what is called a 'bubble raft' floating on the liquid. A straw is good for this. Try it.

59. Keeping a bubble longer

Bubbles usually burst too soon—that is because the air round them dries up their thin skins! If they are floating on water or bubble-liquid, they last longer than up in the air, as you can test for yourself.

If you want to keep a bubble so that you can watch the colours—and it is very interesting to do that—you can guess that you need to keep it in damp air. You get a large glass jar—a big coffee jar is good—and make it wet all over inside. You blow a bubble on top of a plastic coffee beaker wet with bubble liquid, stand the beaker in a saucer, also wet, and put the jar upside-down over the beaker and bubble. With luck, the bubble will

last long enough for you to see the rainbow-coloured rings round it—and to watch them move down it as the bubble gets 'older', and thinner on top! If it didn't work the first time, try again. It isn't *too* easy, but it does work.

60. A bottle full of bubbles

Sometimes in very cold weather you see big bubbles in a half-full milk-bottle, perhaps when someone has shaken it. Try to fill a drinks bottle to the top with bubbles like this: start with an empty bottle, and put in a little water and a few drops of washing-up liquid. Shake it up and down with your hand over the top. The bigger the bubbles you can get, the better. If it doesn't work the first time, you can easily try again, until you have a bottle full of them.

Now look very carefully at their shapes. You know that when you blow bubbles in the open, they are always one shape, and you know exactly what shape that is. These bubbles in the bottle can't be just that shape, can they? Why not? So what sort of shape are they? Look at their sides, where they are pressed against other bubbles. Try to count how many sides one bubble has. Then count for another bubble—and another—and one more. What seems to be the usual number?

You may like to know that this is not just a little game; what you are finding out is important in mathematics and in biology!

The wind, spinners, parachutes, gliders

61. Making a wind

What is the wind made of? Think of ways you could create a small wind. Perhaps you have some little model boats floating in water—and you want them all to sail to the other side of the water-tray. Try just blowing at them. Try fanning them with your hand. Use a piece of stiff card to fan them. Bring your boats back to your side of the water each time, and see which way of making a wind works best.

You might try each way two or three times, to be sure which is the best, and you could think of other ways.

Get a piece of paper, not too soft, and fold a proper fan from it. This may work well; try it.

62. Air from a washing-up liquid bottle

Get hold of an 'empty' washing-up liquid bottle,

and wash it out by squeezing it in and out of water (you will probably get lots of bubbles while you do this—look at them while you have the chance). Now dry the bottle on the outside, and start using it to blow air. Squeeze it so that it blows air against the back of your other hand. Think about the feel of this jet of air: does it feel the same if your hand is wet as it does when your hand is dry?

Next try blowing a jet of air with the squeezy bottle to drive a small model boat across a bowl of water. Can you get the jet to steer the boat as well? What do you see if you just blow the air-jet at the top of the water? Can you make a stronger jet by squeezing with both hands?

If you can find a spare birthday-cake candle, stand it up safely with Blu-Tack or Plasticine, get it lit and see what happens, first when you blow gently at it with your air-jet, and then see if you can blow it out with the strongest jet you can make.

63. Blow through a straw

When someone blows out the candles on their birthday cake, they try to blow them all out at the same time. But can you blow out one candle and leave the others still alight? Get just one birthday-cake candle, a saucer, and a small lump of Plasticine. Make the candle stand up very safely in the middle of the saucer, get it lit and blow through an ordinary milk or lemonade straw at the candle flame. Keep the straw away from the flame, of course. Does it work? Try it again. When you know if it works well or not, put the candle out.

Now just blow through the straw at your hand. Can you feel the air coming through? Blow through your straw at the sail of a little model boat floating in a water-tray. You can see even better what the air does when you use a straw if you blow through it at the top of the water. Don't put the straw end into the water—you know what happens if you do that—just blow at the water from a little way above it. Do it several times, and see if you can draw what it looks like, or tell somebody what it's like.

64. What can you do by just blowing?

Find two fat, heavy books and stand them up side by side, with a narrow space between them—say wide enough for one finger. Blow through the gap. Does this move either of the books?

Now tuck a plastic bag well into the space, with the opening sticking out towards you. Pull the top of the bag together, and blow into it. Can you make your 'blow' make the books (or one book) move? Try it again. Will it work?

Find a round balloon, not blown up, and put it into an empty coffee beaker. Keeping it over the table, for safety, blow into the balloon, and go on blowing until the balloon fills the beaker and bulges over the top edge. Then take hold of the neck of the balloon tightly and lift it. It's safe if you don't let the air out!

In both of these experiments, you blew straight into the plastic bag and the balloon, but the air you blew in pressed sideways as well—and it must have pressed quite hard, mustn't it?

65. Air pumps

Ask your family and friends, and collect as many different kinds of pumps for pumping air as you can. You may be able to get hold of a bicycle pump, a balloon pump, an airbed (Li-Lo) pump and perhaps an emergency car tyre pump (from the boot of somebody's car). Try just pumping with each of these in turn. Feel the air coming out of the nozzle. See if you think the pump which blows hardest is the one which is the hardest to work. Try to find out exactly how each of these pumps works. Do they all have a special valve to keep the air from going backwards? If so, how does it work? If there isn't a valve in the pump, where is it?

If you can borrow a garden pump or syringe, test this too—but make quite sure before you use it that there is no insect-killer spray left in it. Get the owner to wash it out very carefully with water before you try pumping.

66. Vacuum cleaners

Borrow a vacuum cleaner—if at all possible, the kind which lies on the floor. Put it on the table, in a place where the cleaner can be plugged into a socket.

Look at the front end—where the dust goes in. Why does the dust go in?—because air goes in and takes the dust with it! Why does the air go in? This is a bit more difficult to answer. Try it this way. Plug in the cleaner, and switch on—do you *hear* anything? Yes? What sort of electric 'thing' makes this kind of noise? An electric motor? Switch off, and listen; do you hear it slow down before it stops? But what could an electric motor be running inside a vacuum cleaner? Switch on again, and move your hands around near the *back* end of the cleaner. Do you find anything *coming out*? (not dust, of course—there is a kind of filter inside to catch this). But what gets pushed out of the cleaner? Switch off—is this still happening? No? Then the electric motor must work something which pushes air out . . . An electric fan? Think about electric fans you see and feel working in hot weather. Don't they 'blow' air at you? So if the vacuum cleaner blows air out at the back, what is going to happen at the front end? Switch *off*, *unplug*, and see if you can find out more about what happens inside a vacuum cleaner to make it work.

67. Pushing against the air

Choose a day when there is a wind blowing. What is the wind made of? Air, of course—there isn't anything else there. First try just running the way the wind is blowing—with the wind behind you, as people say. Then turn round, and run against the wind. Think about the difference you can feel. Aeroplanes sometimes fly faster than the timetable says, especially from America to Britain. What sort of wind would help them on this route?

Now try pushing against the wind (the air) with a big sheet of stiff cardboard across your front.

And then try with the cardboard beside you, with its edge to the wind. Is this easier? For your third test, try with an open umbrella—against the wind, and then with the wind. You may have done this one often before, but you were not thinking about the air before—only about the rain!

68. Which way is the wind blowing?

If you are out in it, you can *feel* which way the wind is blowing; you can either turn your face to it, or turn your back to it. But if you are indoors, there are other ways of finding out. You can watch the sort of things that are blown and go with the wind: clouds, crisp-bags—even drinks cans. But these all move away till you can't see them.

Instead, you can make a wind-indicator. To get it up in the wind you can use a garden cane, with the bottom end fixed in a big can full of stones or sand. On top you can fix a pennant, or a wind-sock, or a wind-vane. The pennant is a strip of coloured plastic, say from a waste-bin bag, with about 5 to 10 cm of thread between it and the cane. This lets it fly freely in the wind. A wind-sock is just an open-ended tube of nylon, with the wider end held open by thin wire. The wire is tied like the pennant to the cane. A wind-vane is usually a stiff arrow with a big tail. It has to be able to turn round easily; a good way to fix it is with sticky tape to a pen cap, and let this spin on the point of a thin nail taped to the cane. The ends of the arrow must balance one another; use Plasticine, Blu-Tack or paper clips to do this.

69. Rolling with the wind

You can test how hard the wind is blowing by seeing how it rolls things across the playground. Make a test collection of different kinds of balls. Have a football, a table-tennis ball, a blown-up balloon, a sponge ball, and some plastic playground balls. Choose a flat part of the playground, so that they don't roll on their own, and then—on a windy day (but not a wet day) line the balls up across the way the wind is blowing. Stand back, but ready, and see which ball moves first, which moves fastest, which goes furthest, and which only moves a little way or not at all.

You can make a scale of your wind-strength testing balls, numbering them from the most easily blown to the one the wind couldn't move. Try the test again on the same day, to make sure—and then use it on other days to see if the wind is stronger or less strong. (You may have to blow your balloon up again, of course).

70. All sorts of spinners

In the autumn you can often see 'spinners' falling off a sycamore or Long John tree, spinning round as they come down. Some will be double ones, with two wings and two seeds inside the middle part. Probably more will have split, and will only have one wing, but they still spin. Try them if you can find any.

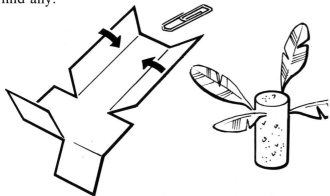

Now make a paper spinner to test. The diagram shows how to cut and fold a strip of paper. Try dropping it with the 'fins' folded down; then put them almost straight up. Bend them both one way; which of these three makes the thing spin most? Which makes it drop most slowly? Does the paper-clip at the bottom make any difference? Try without it. Then try with two!

If you can get hold of a cork and four feathers, all four about the same size, you can make a different spinner by fitting the feathers into holes in the sides of the cork. Make the holes near the end, and sloping up, so that the spinner looks like a badminton shuttlecock. Throw it up, and watch it come down. Turn the feathers at different angles, and get the best results you can.

71. Windmills and turbines

A baby's plastic 'windmill' or 'pin-wheel' has quite a lot of science in it. Borrow one (or the little 'disco' kind, if it hasn't been thrown away) and see how it is made. Why can it spin so easily? Some of these little windmills have a small bead so that there is as little rubbing as possible. Now try *two* ways to make it spin—you can blow at it, like the wind blowing at a windmill (the real kind), or you can make it spin the way the baby usually does. How is that? In any case, the plastic *vanes* catch air which is moving at them.

A turbine is made to spin in the same sort of way. Air, or steam, or water can be made to hit the vanes of a turbine. The turbine spins round, like the baby's windmill, and this makes something else spin very fast—to drive a car or an aeroplane, or perhaps to make electricity. Try making a model turbine which will spin when you blow at it—like this:

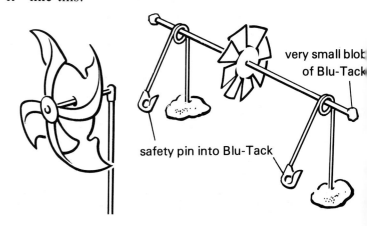

very small blob of Blu-Tack

safety pin into Blu-Tack

72. Plasticine people on parachutes

There are lots of things to find out about the way parachutes work, and you can work in scientific ways to find out. You need a place where you can test a parachute—either by throwing it up and watching it come down again, or by dropping it—say from the top of a staircase (but safely!).

Make several parachutes of different sizes, different materials (better *not* use the handkerchief), and with different-sized little (green?) Plasticine people as 'load'. As a parachute comes down, air gets caught underneath, and has to get away somehow; real parachutes often have a small hole in the middle, so that the air does not rock the parachute by getting out sideways. You could try both kinds.

What makes a parachute drop a *good* one? Is it one which comes down slowly? or comes straight down? or what? Try all the tests you think are worth while—and make a report on them: what you tried and what you found out.

73. Ceiling tiles for kites

Perhaps you know someone who has a few spare polystyrene/styrofoam ceiling tiles. These are so light that they make good little kites. First take a tile out where you have some open space, on a windy day. Flick it across in front of you. See how far you can make it glide—but be careful not to break the edge. These tiles are not very strong.

To make a tile into a kite, you need a long coil of thin string, two fairly light-weight flat buttons, and some thin plastic or crepe paper for tails. Carefully make two holes in the tile, one near the middle and the other about half-way between the first hole and the nearest corner. Thread the string through one hole, then through a button, then through the other button, and then back through the other hole. The buttons should be flat against the tile, on the upper side when it flies, to prevent the string from cutting into it. Tie the string, with

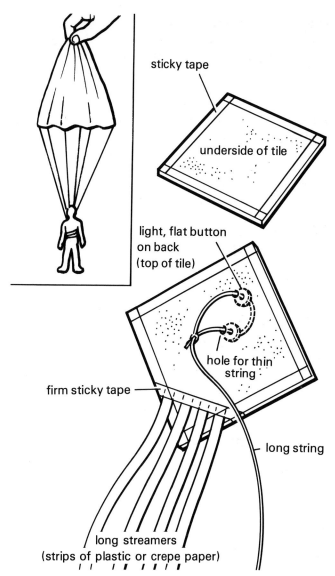

sticky tape

underside of tile

light, flat button on back (top of tile)

hole for thin string

firm sticky tape

long string

long streamers
(strips of plastic or crepe paper)

a good length between the tile and the knot. The kite will not fly without a tail to hold it at the right angle to the wind, so tape long strips to the bottom corner and edges of the tile. You may have to try the string-holes higher up, or more (or less) tail; getting a kite to fly is a real experiment. When it flies, think out where the wind is hitting it. This is what keeps it up in the air.

74. Flying paper gliders

The first thing you need for this is plenty of space. The playground is all right for fun, but any wind spoils the science. The school hall is the best if you can use it, but clear up *every* glider afterwards. Don't use up the school's stock of paper—get an out-of-date telephone book which has not been used much. Once you have seen how to fold a 'standard' glider, there are many scientific tests you can try.

1. Does a heavier glider fly better than a light one? Fold one sheet, two sheets, three sheets . . .

2. Does a small glider fly further than a bigger one? Try a whole page, half a page, a quarter . . .

3. Does a glider fly better with a paper-clip on its nose? or on its undercarriage? or two paper-clips?

4. What happens if you turn up flaps at the back, like the 'spoiler' on a car? Or if you turn them down? or if you turn one up and the other down?

5. Can you make a 'snub-nosed' glider, by folding the tip back underneath before you finish it?

6. Can you make a better glider with sticky tape or gum to hold it together in the middle?

And *how* do you decide which is the best glider?

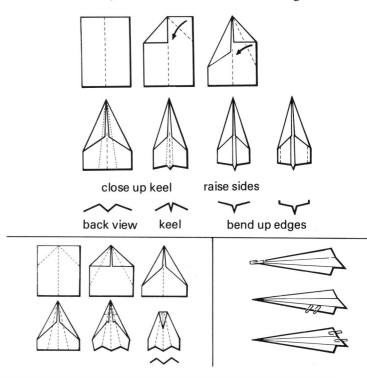

close up keel raise sides

back view keel bend up edges

Water in the air

75. Dry or damp?

How do people know if something—say a bath-towel—is dry or damp? Can they feel it? Sometimes you can feel the difference between damp and dry with your feet—if your socks are wet. . . But with some things you can see by the colour if part is damp and part is dry. Find some pieces of coloured material, and some pieces of coloured paper. Make part of each piece really damp—just not wet enough to drip—and see which shows best the damp part and the dry part.

Some kinds of brown paper and cardboard are good for this, and so is dark-coloured blotting-paper if you can get any. Try white paper, and a stick of chalk, dipping one end in water. Try newspaper.

Can you find anything which simply does not show *any* difference whether it is wet or dry? Some kinds of nylon—perhaps tights? or a bit of an old nylon shirt?—may look just the same wet or dry. Find enough samples to make a little display. They would look good spread out on a black plastic bag.

Afterwards, leave them all to dry. What happens as the damp parts dry up? Can you see which parts were wet even when they are dry again?

76. Puddles in the playground

Everybody knows that when it rains there are puddles in the playground. But they aren't always there. If it's dry the next day, the playground is dry too.

To find out a bit about what happens, go out into the playground with a piece of chalk as soon as it has stopped raining, and draw a line round a puddle, just at the edge of the water. Then look at it every time you can, perhaps at each playtime, and see if the puddle has changed. If it starts raining again, you will have to wait until tomorrow, but you will have the chalk mark to tell you where the water came to. Of course, if the sun comes out as soon as the rain stops, you might be able to put several chalk lines round the puddle—as it dries up.

And if it is dry weather, why not take a beaker of water out, and make a puddle? You could use a neat, measured volume of water—a yogurt-pot full, or an exact 100 millilitres from a measuring jar or jug. How long does it take to dry up? Test this again on another day. . .

77. Breathing on the window

Sometimes there is a little smear or smudge on the window—how can you try to clean it off? Breathe on the glass, and wipe it with a tissue? This often works, doesn't it? But how does it help if you *breathe* on the glass? Try it, first on the window, and then on a mirror. What do you see when you do it? Do you see something more happening if you go on breathing on the same place?

Run your finger down the patch where you have been breathing—what do you get on your finger? This would help to get smudges off the glass, wouldn't it? But where did this wetness come from? It must have come from your breath, mustn't it?

You can find out a bit about why the wetness settled on the glass if you feel the glass with the back of your hand. Does it feel cold? Then breathe gently on the back of the same hand—does your breath feel warm? It should do, shouldn't it—it has just come from a warm place—inside you! Think how often people warm their cold hands by breathing on them. So we could think that perhaps warm *damp* air has to leave some of its dampness (wetness, water) behind when it hits something cold, like the glass.

78. Why do glasses go misty?

Get someone to give you an old pair of glasses that they do not want back. Put the glasses in the fridge for ten minutes (or more). Then just hold them over some hot water in a basin, and watch what happens. You probably guessed what would happen. If you wear glasses yourself, you will know very well what happens if you want to read in the bath, or if you come in from the cold into a warm room or shop.

Now get some more hot-bath-hot water in the bowl and dip the glasses in this water for a minute or so; take them out, dry them quickly with a tissue, and hold them over the hot water as you did the first time. The first time the glasses were very cold; this time they are warm. What difference does it make, or doesn't it make any difference? Can you think why?

79. A cold tin in a warm room

Find a clean, shiny tin—a soup or a baked-bean tin—and a clean, shiny glass jar about the same size—perhaps a jam-jar. Pour a little cold water into each, and then drop in a few ice cubes, enough to fill the tin and the jar just over half full. Look at the outsides of both tin and jar after five or ten minutes. Run your finger down the side. What do you discover?

If you can get a big, shiny can, say the big instant-coffee kind, with a lid, try this puzzle on somebody. Don't let them know what you are doing, but put a little cold water and then a lot of ice cubes into the tin. Then put the lid on—and after, say, a quarter of an hour show them the tin and ask them if they can guess without touching it what you have done.

What is there on the outside of the cold tin? And where must it have come from? (It can't have come from inside the tin, can it?)

80. Water into the air—and out again

Find a clear container, perhaps a glass pudding-basin or a plastic lunch-box. Put some hot water in the bottom, and cover the top loosely with one layer of a plastic bag or clingfilm. Then put a rubber band or a strip of sticky tape round to hold the covering, and place one or two ice-cubes on it, so that they are on the plastic over the hot water.

After a few minutes, look at the underside of the plastic bag or clingfilm. It will have been cooled by the ice, but the air underneath it will have been hot and damp. What has the coldness done?

Where else have you seen the same sort of thing happening?

81. Making a sample of mist

This needs a really clear beaker or jar, some hot water, a tea-strainer, and an ice-cube or two. You put the hot water into the beaker, rest the tea-strainer on top of it, and put the ice into the strainer. The ice cools the air in the top of the beaker, while the hot water is making the air at the bottom hot and damp. Watch the space in the middle of the beaker. You can see what happens even better if you can put it in sunshine, or shine a projector or torch beam through the beaker.

Think about mist over rivers, lakes and the sea; there aren't any ice-cubes there, but cold air and warmer moist air do meet—and mist happens.

Ice and snow

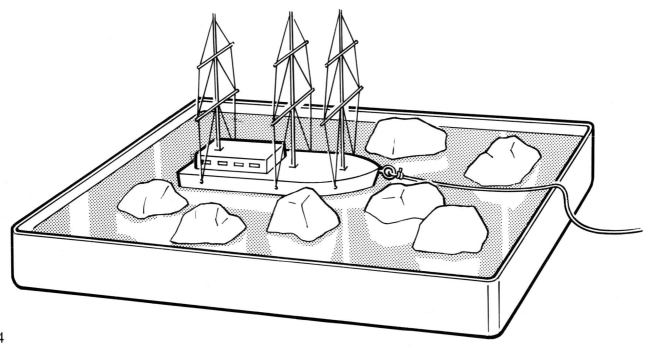

82. Ice cubes and icebergs

Get a water tray, or a big baking tin. Half-fill it with cold water, and then tip in as many ice cubes as you can. Put a small model boat in the middle. It could be one from the bath or, even better, a boat you have made out of wood. This is your *Polar Explorer* among the icebergs. Tie a thread to the bow of the boat, and pull it gently across the water. Watch the icebergs, as well as the boat, and think about ships in the Arctic or Antarctic.

83. Freeze a model pond

Get a bowl which will just go into the freezing part of the fridge. Fill it about half full with cold water, and put it into the freezing compartment very carefully. Now have a quick look at it every ten minutes; you don't need to take it right out until there is some ice there. Where is the ice when your pond just begins to freeze? This is a very important result—think about sliding on ponds, and what can happen.

Put the bowl back for another ten or twenty minutes. Look again, and feel the ice with your finger.

Some ponds have fish in them; ice over the top will stop air getting to them. If you want to break the ice on a pond, crack the edge upwards. Hitting the ice can kill the fish with the shock.

84. Looking at snowflakes

The pictures of snowflakes in books, looking like tiny white six-pointed stars, are not always like the flakes which fall in the garden or the playground. Ordinary snowflakes are often made of several small ones sticking rather untidily together—and as soon as you catch them, especially if you breathe on them, they start to melt. Can you think how to keep them a bit longer? Try this, for example: when it starts to snow, get a piece of black plastic (rubbish bag?) or black paper, or even black fabric (velvet

is the very best!) and lay it on top of the tray of ice-cubes in the fridge. After a few minutes it will be really cold, so you take the whole tray—ice-cubes, plastic or paper or velvet on top—out into the snow, and catch some flakes on it as they fall. This will give you a much better chance to look at them, even with a magnifier if you want to, before they melt. You can see how it works—and as the flakes are white, the black stuff makes them show up.

85. Squeezing snow, squeezing ice

Everybody knows how to make a snowball—you just get a big handful of snow and squeeze it. What happens? The snow sticks together. If you want a bigger one, you squeeze some more snow on the outside of your first snowball. If you can get some snow, try it. You may know what happens if you go on squeezing hard for a long time—you get a very hard snowball. In fact, it isn't a *snow*ball any longer, it has turned into an iceball.

Now get a thick duster or cloth, and two ice cubes. Put the ice cubes together, flat side to flat side, wrap the cloth round them, and press them together as hard as you can. Keep it up for two or three minutes, and then unwrap the ice. Think about the way you make snow stick together into a snowball. Does the same thing happen with ice? After all, snow is a kind of ice, isn't it?

86. Find out more about snow

If it snows overnight, make the most of it next morning.

1. Look for tracks—made by people, birds, the caretakers' dog or cat. See who made which—you could even measure and draw them. Tread several times around the same place—you may get a 'pad' of hard snow turning into ice on your shoe-soles. This can be very slippery; it happens under horses' hoofs and car tyres. Think—if you go on squeezing a snowball, it turns into an 'iceball'.

2. Measure the depth of the snow in different places.

You may find a small snowdrift—against a fence or a wall. How does it get deeper there? Which way is the wind blowing? Which way is the sun shining?

3. *If* the sun is shining, try this: get two pieces of plastic (or paper), one white and one black. Put them down flat on the snow, side by side. Hold them down with stones at the corners. Which do you think will catch more of the heat from the sun? Look under both after an hour, and again at the end of the morning. Is there any difference? You may be lucky!

4. Scoop up a beaker of snow, and scrape it off so that it is level on top—just full. Take it back indoors and let it melt. How much water comes from the snow? What must have been between the snowflakes?

87. Snowball and snowman

A small snowball is easy to make when it has just snowed. How do you make it bigger? Just squeeze some more snow on the outside. It's the squeezing that makes it stick, isn't it? Now, for a good snowman you need a huge snowball for his body—how can you make it big enough? People usually do it by starting with a snowball they can pick up and then rolling it along on more snow; it is heavy enough to squeeze the snow underneath it and make that stick on. Try for yourself when there is enough snow—you may need others to help when Snowman's body gets really large. Now, what about his head, made the same way—how do you make it stay on? Perhaps by putting it on the body, with a cloth over the top so that you can pull it down by the corners to press it till it sticks.

Why is the 'rolling' method not good for making snowballs to throw? Look at your big snowman-body: it is probably not very clean white snow—bits of grit and even small stones get picked up as you roll it. If you can make several big snowballs, leave them in a corner somewhere and see how long they last after the snow on the ground has gone. Can you leave two of the same size, one in a sunny place

and the other near it but in the shade? A good test with two more, both of the same size, would be to leave them side by side, but one with a black plastic rubbish bag right over it, and stones or bricks to hold the bag down. Look at them both twice a day!

88. Ice-cube competition

It is easy to think of ways to melt an ice cube quickly—you can hold it in your hand, or put it under the hot tap, or. . . try to think of five ways to melt it fast. But now think of ways to stop an ice cube from melting, without a fridge or a freezer. Try some ways for yourself—for example, wrapping it in different things to keep it cold.

Have a competition with one or two friends, all starting with the same-sized ice cubes. Which of you can keep a bit of ice the longest? (You will all risk getting a bit wet, but it will be good science.)

89. Ice cubes in water

Have a few ice cubes ready in the tray. Wrap the tray in a whole newspaper if you want to keep the cubes really cold. Half-fill a clear jar or a clear plastic beaker with cold water, and drop in one cube. Watch what happens when it hits the water; then watch where it stays. Can you see anything happening underneath the ice cube? You may be able to see more if you put the jar or beaker in sunshine, or if you shine a torch through the water.

Next, tip this lot away, and have two jars or beakers side by side, one half full of cold water, and the other half full of hot water. Drop an ice cube into each jar, both at the same time. You can guess what will happen. Is your guess right? Can you time another pair of ice cubes like this, to see which goes first?

90. Coloured ice cubes

When nobody else wants ice for anything, try making some coloured cubes. You could use a blackcurrant drink, or orange juice, or you could colour some water. The colours people use for cake icing, red or blue or green, would do very well. If you have another ice-cube tray, why not put milk in one or two of the spaces and see if you can make milk cubes? Put the tray (or trays) in the freezing part of the fridge for an hour or two.

When your coloured cubes are solid ice, take one out and drop it into plain water in a clear glass or beaker. Watch carefully what happens. You will be able to see best if you look through the glass from the side, with your head almost on the table.

Try the same thing with a bit of a coloured ice lolly. Just for a surprise, why not try making tea or coffee cubes? With or without milk?

91. When the ice melts. . .

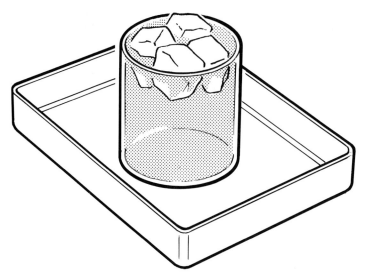

Stand a beaker in a tray or a deep plate, and fill it nearly full of water. Then carefully put one or two ice cubes into the water. Next, very carefully fill the beaker right up to the top. If you use a small jug or a teapot, you can do this without letting the water overflow. Now, the ice cube will be floating, with a bit sticking up in the air. What is going to happen as it melts? Watch and find out.

92. Do ice cubes get heavier or lighter when they melt?

The best way to find the mass of ice cubes is to use a plastic beam balance. Pile several ice cubes into one of the plastic 'buckets', and balance them with anything you like. You can find their real mass if you have 'weights', but it doesn't matter for this experiment. You are just going to find out if the mass of the ice changes and, if so, which way. Before the ice melts, guess what will happen. Then when the cubes have turned to water, see if your guess was right. Did the ice get heavier as it melted, or did it get lighter, or did it stay the same mass?

93. A 'weighing ice and water problem'

Start with a balance that has plastic pans or 'buckets', and half-fill one bucket with water. (The bucket may be called a scoop or a tub—it doesn't matter.) Find the mass of this water or balance it with something in the other bucket. Now put a few ice cubes into the water. They float—do you think they will make the bucket heavier, or will it have the same mass as before you put them in? Test your guess by the balance. Were you right?

Now let the ice melt in the water. When it has all melted, there won't be anything floating, sticking up out of the water. What do you think will have happened to the mass of the water with the melted ice in it? Find out if your guess was right this time. It probably was.

94. Salted ice cubes?

Get two clear beakers or jars, and count the same number of ice cubes into each—say three or four cubes. Put them together, and into one beaker or jar pour enough salt to cover the cubes quite thickly. Then watch—and listen—to see what happens. Do you hear anything from either of them?

Leave both beakers for a few minutes, and look again. Are the ice cubes melting? Are they melting at the same rate, or is one lot of ice melting faster than the other? See which one finishes first, or if they both melt at the same time.

People sometimes sprinkle salt on their front paths in frosty weather—can you see a reason why they do this?

95. How cold are melting ice cubes?

Melting ice cubes feel cold to your fingers, of course, but you really need a thermometer to find out how cold they are. The usual kind of thermometer which hangs on the classroom wall will do quite well. It usually has a wooden back, which ought not to get wet, but you can simply put the whole thermometer into a plastic bag, wrapping the extra folds round the back so that the tube and the scale are easily seen. Get a beaker of cold water and several ice cubes in it, and put the thermometer so that the bottom end is well into the water and ice. Look at the temperature every five or ten minutes, until all the ice has melted. What was the coldest temperature you found?

Now, start again with a little water at the bottom, stand the thermometer in it, pile ice cubes round it, and then tip in some salt on top of and all round the ice. Again, watch the temperature shown by the thermometer. Do you get the same result as you did with plain ice? Make a note of the lowest (coldest) temperature you found this time—with ice and salt.

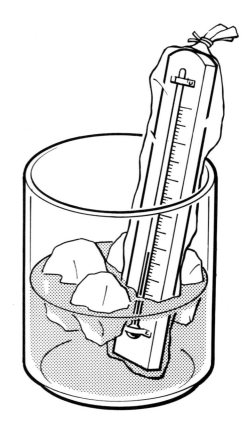

96. The top of the ice cube

Put some cold water in an ice-cube tray. Look at the top of the water in the spaces—it looks very ordinary. Put the tray carefully in the freezing compartment of the fridge, and leave it until the water is frozen. When you take the tray out again, look at the tops of the ice cubes. Do they all look just as the water did?

Now try this another way. Fill a cup or a beaker with cold water as full as you can, and put this in to freeze. When you take it out, look at the top of the ice, and think about what has happened.

Next time you have, or a friend has, an ice-lolly, look at the ice just round the stick. Did it freeze flat, or is there a hump round the stick?

What seems to happen just before an ice cube or a lolly goes solid?

97. Can you make your own ice-lolly?

Try this and see if it works: first of all get a small, clear plastic beaker to make your lolly in (the kinds called Glacier, or Party Cup, are good). Mix a few drops of food colouring with water, and pour it in. If you put a paper lid on the beaker, you can stand a lolly stick through a hole in the lid.

Ice cubes don't fit round things you want to cool, so smash up some cubes by wrapping them in a whole folded newspaper, putting the 'parcel' on the floor, and hitting it with something hard which won't break—say half a brick. Open the news-paper, scoop up broken ice into a tin or bowl, pour quite a lot of salt on to the ice, and quickly settle your beaker of coloured water into a space in the middle of the ice and salt mixture. Leave the whole thing for about ten minutes—look at it—put it back for another ten minutes—and so on, till nothing more happens. Nobody can say just how long this will be; it partly depends on how cold it was when you began.

Ice mixed with salt is called a 'freezing mixture'; is this a good name for it?

If you had some snow, you wouldn't need to break up the ice cubes, would you? You could just use snow instead.

98. Frozen Coke?

If you have tried freezing coloured water, or just plain water, you will have seen that it seems to bulge at the top when it freezes.

Canned drinks are also coloured water, with a taste, so try one—in its can. Get a nice, thick duster and a new can of your usual drink. Roll the can up in the duster, and put it in the freezing compartment of the fridge. Leave it there for a day, or overnight, and then take it out and see if anything has happened.

Did you guess that anything would happen? Did it? Pull the ring, and see what you have got in the can. What does this experiment tell you about freezing water, or at least about freezing a drink in a can?

Mixing things with water

99. Instant coffee

For this activity you only need a clear beaker, a teaspoon, a little instant coffee powder or granules (much less than the spoonful), and water to fill the beaker just over half full.

Put a *very* little coffee into the water, and stir. What happens to the coffee? What happens to the water? Can you see that the coffee is still in the beaker? Tip in a little more coffee, and stir again. Look at the water—can you see bits of coffee floating about in it? Or does the coffee mix so well with the water that all you can see of the coffee is the colour? Now put in the rest of the instant coffee and give it a good stir. Look at the bottom of the beaker—is there any coffee (powder or granules) lying on the bottom? Hold the beaker up to the light. Can you see anything through your 'black coffee'?

If something mixes so well with water that there is nothing left on the bottom, and you can see through the mixture—if it is *clear*, even though it may be coloured, then the mixture is a *solution*.

The stuff which mixed with the water in a solution is called a *soluble substance*; perhaps you can find the word 'soluble' on the coffee label?

100. How weak can coffee be?

Start with a white cup or a clear beaker. Fill it nearly full of water, and then drop in a very little instant coffee—one granule or a tiny pinch of the powder. A dry straw would be a good scoop to pick up such a little coffee powder. Stir the water. Is there enough coffee to colour the water? Hold a piece of white paper behind the clear beaker to see the colour better. If you are using a cup, try to have another cup exactly like it with only water in it, so that you can see if there is any difference. If the mixture looks quite brown, tip some away and add more water. Try to get the palest brown you can still see—the weakest coffee you can make!

Very weak coffee is a very *dilute solution* of coffee in water. Can you taste the coffee in the water when it is as dilute as this?

101. Coffee with milk

For this you need three clear jars or beakers, a stirrer (or a teaspoon, of course), a very little instant coffee (powder or granules) and a little milk.

Fill two jars about half full of water, and stir coffee into one of them, and milk into the other. Try to see through each of them—perhaps to see if you can read letters on paper behind the jars. One of the mixtures will look clear, even if it is coloured. The other one will look 'thick'.

Now pour both the coffee and the milk into the third jar; watch, and then stir the mixture. What colour is it? How thick does it look? Would you say that it looks about 'half-way' between the coffee and the milk you started with? Many

mixtures in science are like this—a bit like each of the things you put into the mixture.

102. Sugar in water

Try to get small 'samples' of four different kinds of sugar: ordinary (granulated or lump) sugar, icing sugar, the coarse kind of sugar, called preserving sugar, that people use for making jam or marmalade, and some kind of brown sugar. Now you need four clear beakers or small jars about half full of water, and teaspoons.

Put a spoonful of each of the first three kinds—the white ones—into their beakers (or jars), and give each lot the same number of stirs. This is to make the experiment 'fair'. After, say, five stirs each, look at the bottom of the water, and see if there is any sugar lying on the bottom. Which kind of sugar disappeared into the water first? Which kind took the longest to go? If there is still any sugar left in any jar, stir again. Can you get it all to disappear into the water? Is the water still clear?

Now put a spoonful of brown sugar into the last jar, and stir this. Can you get all the sugar to disappear into the water? How do you know that it is really mixed with the water? Can you tell in two different ways?

103. Making sugar syrup

This is an experiment you can test by tasting it at the end. You need a clear beaker or a cup, about half full of warm (or even hot) water; you also want a teaspoon and about a cupful of sugar. This can be any kind—white or brown.

You start by putting two or three spoonfuls of sugar into the water; watch for a minute or two before you begin to stir—you can see that the sugar is beginning to mix into the water and *dissolve* even without any help. Then stir carefully, and when almost all the sugar has *dissolved* into the water, put in some more. Stir again. When there is some sugar at the bottom which does not go even when you stir, the water has been turned into a sugar syrup. With the teaspoon, take a little out from the top and taste it. You can't see sugar in the water at the top of the mixture, but you have a good way of knowing that it's there. With brown sugar you can see it *and* taste it—that's two ways of knowing.

104. How much sugar dissolves?

This is not a scientific question, is it? You need to know how much water there is, and whether it is hot or cold water, to begin with. So think of ways to make the experiment more scientific. An easy way would be to use sugar cubes—all alike—to measure how much sugar you use; you could weigh some and find out how many grams one cube weighs. Then you could measure out the water; quite a few small bottles, for shampoo and so on, have the volume the bottle holds marked on the side or on the bottom.

Now, put a measured volume of cold water from a marked bottle into a clear beaker or a cup. Beside this put another beaker (or cup) with the same measured volume of hot water in it. Then start by putting a sugar cube into each lot of water, and stirring the same number of times for each. Add another cube when the first one has gone—but watch to see that there isn't a lot of sugar left at the bottom. When one lot of water will not take any more sugar, stop adding sugar cubes to that one and make a note of how many dissolved in it. Go on with the other lot until no more will dissolve. The number of cubes will give you a rough but useful answer. Weighing and measuring will make it more scientific.

Which dissolved more sugar, the hot or the cold water?

105. Very strong salt water

Half-fill a clear beaker with water, and add two or three teaspoonfuls of salt. Stir the mixture. It will probably look a bit cloudy, but this does not matter.

Look at the salt at the bottom. When most of it has gone (into the water) put in some more, and stir again. Do this until there is some salt at the bottom which stays there, however much you stir.

Now dip the tip of your finger into the water and taste it. A very strong mixture, like this very strong salt water, is a *concentrated solution*; this one is a concentrated solution of salt in water. Stir it again, several times. If you really cannot get any more salt to dissolve in the water, you have made a *saturated solution* (of salt in water).

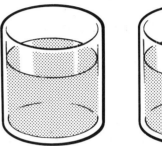

106. Mixtures—thick or clear?

Start with a row of clear beakers or 'party cups', or small, clean jam-jars. Put the same amount of water into each one. Now collect four teaspoons, one to stir each lot of water, and a teaspoonful of sugar for one, flour for the next, salt for the third, and either dried milk powder or instant mashed potato, or cornflour, for the fourth pot.

Put the powders into the water, and stir. After a minute or two, stop and look carefully at each mixture. Is there a really clear one? If so, which? Is there a really thick-looking one? If so, which? What can you say about the others? Make a list, from the 'clearest' to the 'thickest' of your mixtures.

Now let them all stand still for an hour or so, and look again. Is there something more to say about what you see?

A mixture which stays 'thick-looking' is called a *suspension*—the stuff you put in stays suspended, or 'held up'.

L. I. H. E.
THE MARKLAND LIBRARY
STAND PARK RD., LIVERPOOL, L16 9JD

41

Separating mixtures; things which will not mix

107. Salt water drying up

Mix or shake up some salt with some water—it does not matter how much of each, but you only need a few drops of the mixture. Let it settle for a few minutes. Next, if you can, find a dark brown plastic lid from an empty instant-coffee jar, and take out the card lining. Pour out a little of the salty water into the plastic lid, and put it in a safe place (but not in the fridge). Don't cover it up, but just leave it, perhaps until tomorrow.

Will you get the salt back? Why do you think a dark brown lid will make it easier for you to find out than a white saucer would? What do you find in the lid when the water has dried up? Look in the lid with a magnifier—this will make it more interesting.

108. Drinking water on a desert island

Desert islands, and others such as the Channel Islands, are often short of fresh water, though they have plenty of sea. But sea water is bad for people, and for most plants and land animals. So how can one get fresh water out of salt water? Can we filter out the salt? Guess! But then try it—never trust a guess without trying it, if you are a scientist. And this one is very easy to test—just mix some salt into some water, and then pour the salty water into a coffee-filter paper sitting in a mug. Does the salt come through in the water?

Now—in the sunshine of the island, a lot of sea water will dry up. Does it take the salt with it? Guess again. And now see if there is a way to get the water back after it has dried up. You may have seen gardeners' plastic cloches, 'tunnels' or 'propagators' with water running down inside the plastic. This is a way to catch back water which has 'dried up'.

Make some strong salt water, put it in a flat dish (polystyrene or foil?), cover it with a plastic or plastic-bag 'tent', and catch what runs down inside—without letting it run back into the salty water. You can invent a 'plastic-bag tent', stuck with bits of Blu-Tack round the edge of a bigger dish (or tray) with the salt-water one in the middle. Put it all on a sunny window-sill (remember the sunny island) and look next morning. You could even dare to taste what you have collected—there will not be enough to drink!

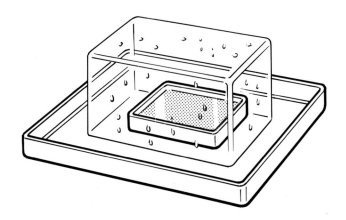

109. Gettings things out of water

We often need to get quite big things out of water—say boiled potatoes or beans. Some people hold the potatoes back with the saucepan lid while they pour the water away, others use a colander or a kitchen strainer. For chips we use a wire basket, because we want to keep the frying oil.

Make a 'test-mixture' for yourself by mixing up some sawdust and water coloured with paint or food-colouring. Try all the different strainers you can borrow—a tea or coffee strainer, a colander, a soup strainer and so on. Which works best?

Now make one or two strainers—say from a piece of old curtain-net or tights nylon. How are you going to hold these up? You could stretch the stuff over the top of a jar, and put a rubber band round. Can you think of better ways to strain the mixture? Can you get everything out of the water that you put in?

110. Keeping the coffee grounds out of the cups

When people make coffee from coffee beans (not from 'instant' coffee), the beans are ground up into very small hard pieces; these are the coffee grounds.

There are several ways of keeping the grounds out of the cups. Think of some ways: you can pour very slowly and carefully, leaving the bits at the bottom of the pot (this is called 'decanting'), or you can use a coffee strainer, and so on. But one way seems to be the best—using a *filter*.

Can you get a few of the ready-made coffee filter papers from someone who uses them? The biggest size you can! These are in a kind of funnel-shape. You can either open them out and fit them into ordinary plastic funnels, or you can even get somebody to hold one while you pour your mixture into it and the water runs through into a jar or beaker. Find out about what stays in the paper and what goes through. Think what the papers are made for—so what *has* to go through?

When any kind of coloured water comes through one of these filters, does the water look thick or does it look clear? This is very important in science, as well as in good coffee!

111. Water and melted candlewax

Get a small bowl or soup-plate of cold water and a short candle or a night-light. Carefully light the candle (or nightlight) and let it burn for a minute or two. Why?—to give the flame a chance to melt some wax at the bottom of the wick. Then tilt the candle over the water, and let some wax run out. Watch very carefully, as soon as you have put the candle back safely where nobody will get burnt by it.

Watch the wax being cooled by the water: you can see something happening as it sets—several things, in fact. Does the wax sink or float? What does this tell you? Is the melted wax clear or cloudy-looking? Does it stay the same, or change? What shape is the top of the drop or blob—bulging, flat or shrunk-looking? Does the shape of the top stay the same from the moment it hits the water to the time it has set hard? This should tell you something too. You may remember that ice-cubes and lollies have a hump on top, because water gets a little bigger as it freezes. What about candlewax?

If you missed anything, tip a little more melted wax on to the water, and watch again. Last of all, stir up the water and the drops of wax together. Can you make the wax dissolve into the water?

112. Wax rubbings and water paint

Make a small rubbing with a bit of candle, or with a nightlight taken out of its case. You could do a rubbing of a bit of a manhole cover, or a stiff leaf, or a larger coin. Then paint over the paper with fairly watery paint; it can be a dark colour, but not too thick. Hang it up to dry. Can you see if wax and water(paint) will mix? Try a few more rubbings—they will probably get better as you do more.

Some people decorate eggshells with a pattern drawn in wax, and then paint afterwards. It is also the way batik patterns are put on fabric. If you use

a coloured wax crayon instead of the white candle-wax you will have a two-colour design.

113. Will oil and water mix?

The oil in oil-stoves is paraffin, and it is usually coloured, so it will be easy to see if it mixes with water. Look for a bottle with a really good stopper or screw cap, because paraffin gets out of most bottles and makes everything smell. Mark on the side of the bottle about one-third and two-thirds of the height. Then pour in one-third of coloured paraffin oil. On top of this, pour in the same volume of water. Close the bottle tightly, and shake the two liquids together. Then stand the bottle down (on newspaper, just in case. . .) and watch.

You may have tried putting a candle in water; the candle is made of paraffin wax—there should be some connection.

114. Oil on water

For this you need a plate or dish of water, and a very little oil; it can be cooking oil or oil-can oil. Drip a few drops of oil on the top of the water. Look at the drops as they hit the water, and again when they have settled. Compare them with the drops of candlewax on water.

Look at a bottle of ordinary milk (not homogenized) at home or in a shop. What is on top? Why do you think there is anything special about what people call 'the top of the milk'?

If you can, borrow a 250-gram packet of butter, in its paper or foil. Feel the weight—will it float or sink in water? Ask other people. Then test your (and their) guess by putting the pack of butter into a bowl of clean water, and see what happens.

Plants and water

115. Flowers need water

Pick a few weeds that have flowers on them. Put some of them with their stems in water in a jar, and some others in the same sort of jar without any water. Leave both jars side by side all day, or even until the next morning. You can see which plants are all right and which are not, and you know what made the difference.

Now try to find out if the plants which have water take any of it: you can use the same two jars, both alike, and fill them both to exactly the same level. Put a bunch of flowers—weeds again if you like—into one jar, but leave the other jar with just water in it. Put them side by side, and leave them alone for about two days. How can you find out if the plants really took any water? If you lift their stems out carefully, letting the drips go back into the jar, you can look at the water levels of the water in the two jars, and see if the plants seem to have taken any water out, or not.

You guessed before you started this test, didn't you? And got the right answer? But scientists always test their guesses; some people do guess wrong sometimes.

116. If plants need water, what happens to it?

If plants kept all the water they take in inside themselves, what would happen? Think about ourselves too—if we kept inside ourselves all the things we drink—the water, tea, milk, lemonade and so on, we would be like balloons filled with water. But we know how *we* get rid of the water we don't want inside. What do plants do?

Try this experiment, and see if it tells you anything: find a nice bushy, leafy weed or a twig with plenty of leaves on it. Put its head into a plastic bag without any holes, and fix the closure round the stem. Then put the bottom end of the twig or plant in water in a jar, and leave it on a window-sill—in the sun if there is any. Look at it two or three times during the day, and again the next morning. What does it tell you about the water the plant or twig has been taking out of the jar?

The scientific name for what has been happening is *transpiration*.

117. How many peas on a coin?

All you need for this experiment is a coin, some dried peas (for cooking or left over from the garden), a little water and a little patience. It has quite a lot of science in it, and other experiments rather like it will tell you more.

Put the coin down flat, and see how many dry peas you can fit on top of it in a single layer—no piling up. Count them, and write down the number. Tip them off, and do it again—more than once, if you are being very scientific—or get somebody else to do it once or twice. Make a note of the number of dry peas every time.

Now put the peas in water, and leave them for at least a day. Overnight would do very well. Tip the water away, dry off the drips of water (rolling the peas on newspaper would be a good way) and see how many of your soaked peas you can fit on top of the coin. Again, do this more than once, or get somebody else to do it too. Can you get as many as you did the first time on top of your coin? Has anything happened? Can you see anything about the look of the peas now which helps to explain what you find out? Remember to write down how many soaked peas you got on the coin, to compare with the numbers of the dry ones at the beginning.

118. Soaking dried peas

You can sometimes get dried peas for cooking from a shop, or perhaps a gardener has some left over from the year before last. Look at them—they are hard, rather small, and often wrinkled-looking and shrunk.

Fill an eggcup neatly with these dried peas, and stand it in the middle of the lid of an empty tin, such as a biscuit tin. Now carefully pour water into the eggcup (from a jug or teapot. . .) until the water just fills it to the brim. The whole thing will have to be left somewhere just out of people's way while the peas get soaked—it takes some hours.

But as soon as the peas really begin to get soaked thoroughly, you will know about it! Think what may happen as they soak up water. . . what could be the point of standing the eggcup on the lid of the big, empty tin? Guess, and then see if your guess works.

119. Chips with water?

No, not to eat, though the chips can be fried and eaten afterwards if you like!

You need a long (Irish) potato (raw), a knife, a ruler, and some cold water in a dish.

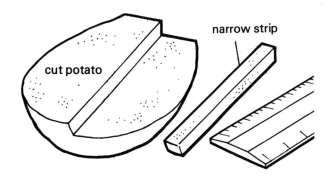

Carefully cut a few nice long strips from the middle of the potato; they can be thinner than the usual size, but get them as long as you can. Cut the ends off square, and make at least four all the same length. Measure these along your ruler, and write down the exact length.

Now put two right into the water, flat on the bottom of the dish. Put out two of the same length on newspaper on the table, so that they drain and begin to dry up.

After about a quarter of an hour, pick up two strips by one end, one strip from the water and one from the table. Do you notice any difference? Did you think there would be any difference? Why?

After about half an hour, or longer, measure all the strips again very carefully. Has the water made any difference? Check the 'feel', the stiffness, and the length of all the 'chips'. What could have happened to make the differences?

120. Dandelion stalks and water

Think about a dandelion stalk for a minute or two. It has to hold up a head of many very small flowers (called florets, one to each 'petal'), and even when the wind is strong it does not seem to blow dandelions over. Sometimes there may be a large bumble-bee on top as well—though dandelions don't need bees, the florets make seeds without any help.

How much help do the stalks get from water, though? Pick a few soft hollow stalks, put all but one quickly in a jar of water, and leave one without water. As this one dries up, the difference shows.

Now try this: with a sharp knife (and care) slit a stalk into long, narrow strips—from the bottom to the flower-head if you can. Leave one or two strips on the table, und put the rest in water in a plate. Watch them. Look again after half an hour.

To think out what goes on, remember that the *outside* skin of the stalk is tough, and almost water-proof; the *inside* layer of the stalk is soft and sponge-like. If you look carefully and think hard, you can explain what happens. Check by taking some strips out and letting them dry up a bit: you could put the first drying ones into water, if they have not got too dry. Can this test work both ways?

121. Water for leaves

We all know when flowers in a vase, or soft leaves for salad, have been left without water. They flop and go limp. Try this with a juicy kind of leaf, say a radish or salad leaf. Sometimes you can rescue the leaves by giving them water—and sometimes it's too late. But we all know how to give them water—by putting the stalks in the water. That means that the water has to get to the rest of the leaf somehow.

To find out more about it, get two or three stalks of celery or balsam, with as much of the leaves still on the top as you can. Greengrocers often sell leafy celery. Busy Lizzie (balsam) works well.

Stand one pale stalk in water, and another in water which you have coloured with food-colouring—perhaps red or blue. After a day or two,

look carefully at the stalk to see if you can find the colour. Then cut off a short piece from the bottom end of each stalk and compare what you see.

If you have a third stalk, split it up from the bottom for about 10 centimetres, making two equal half-stalks joined for the top part. Put two coffee beakers side by side, with red-coloured water in one and blue or some other colour in the other. Stand the stalk so that one half is dipping into each colour of water. Leave it again for a day or two, and see what happens. You can easily guess, but test your guess just the same.

Breathing

122. Breathing in and out

In a crowded lift, sometimes a person says 'Breathe in!' Does it help? Try. Put your hands round your ribs, and breathe in and out two or three times. What do you feel happening? Get a tape-measure (or even a piece of string, if there is no tape-measure) and put it round your chest. Hold one end with one hand, and pull gently with the other hand so that the string shows just how far it is round you. Do this while you breathe out, and find a way to mark the string where it just touched the other end. Of course, if you have a tape-measure, look at the marking on it.

Now do the same thing when you have just taken a big breath in. How much further round are you with a big breath inside? This is called your *chest expansion*.

Get these two lengths—of the string or of the tape—two or three times. You may find that the second time you try it you make your chest expand more, because you are trying harder! It does not matter how fat or slim you are—the thing to measure is the difference between 'breath out' and 'breath in' measurements.

123. Ribs and bucket-handles

To breathe in, we have to make room inside our chests for more air to come in. We do it in two ways, and one of them is by moving our ribs.

We can make a simple model like this: find two buckets, both alike, with handles which hang down a bit. Put one inside the other, and measure across the top. Now get someone to lift both handles to the level of the tops of the buckets—and measure across buckets and their handles. Write down both widths: handles down, handles up. What do you find out?

Next, take hold of the bucket handles yourself, and raise and lower them as you breathe in (up) and out (down). Keep in time, and think about the way your ribs are moving to make more room inside as you breathe in, and then less room as you breathe out again. You can see why this experiment is called 'ribs and bucket-handles'.

Watch the breathing movements of a horse, or a sleeping cat; or put your hands round your dog's ribs and feel the movements.

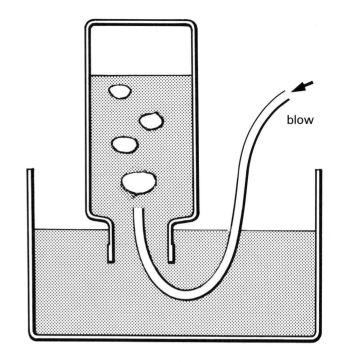

124. How much air can you breathe out?

Let's start with one important fact—nobody can breathe out all the air there is inside them, inside their lungs. Why not? Because our chests won't go flat like a plastic bag; our ribs keep quite a large space inside our chests. But get a big plastic bag, pull up the top to make a small opening to blow into, and then flatten the bag on the table. Now blow into the bag, and see how much air you can blow into it. Close the bag with a wire closure.

Can you think of a way to let this 'breathed-out air' go into a big jar of water turned upside down in water in an old fish-tank, or in water in the sink? This would give you an idea of how much air you breathed out.

125. Measure the air you breathe out

People in training for athletics or space-flights can measure the air they breathe out with something like a gas-meter, with little wheels going round as they blow. We can do it in a simpler way, so that we can see how much air we breathe out. You need a large fish-tank about half full of water, a large plastic sweet-jar (if you can get one from an old-fashioned sweet shop) and a piece of plastic tubing. If you cannot get the sweet-jar, try for a really big lemon-drink bottle—perhaps the kind with a hollow handle. The 1½ litre kind is not big enough.

Fill the jar or bottle full to the top with water

and screw the top on. Then turn it upside-down in the water in the tank (or in the sink, if you haven't got a tank). Unscrew the top, under water—the water can't come out because air can't get in. Now put one end of the tube in your mouth and the other into the bottle or jar—still keeping the neck of the jar under water. Take a big breath—through your nose—and blow steadily (not too fast) into the bottle. You may need someone else to hold the jar for you, and you may need to try the whole experiment a second time. If you do, start from the beginning again, with the jar full right up.

Now you can see how much air you have blown out of your lungs. To measure it, screw the top on the jar again, still under water, take it out, and fill up with water from a measuring beaker, counting how many measures it takes. This will measure how much space your breath filled up.

126. Make a model lung

For this simple model you need a big plastic sponge—the kind used for cleaning the car will do well—and a small plastic bag to put the sponge in.

Pull the mouth of the plastic bag together round a short cardboard roll, and fix it with a rubber band. You can squeeze the bag to make the lung 'breathe out', and you can make it blow bubbles in water. Drop the model lung on water—without drowning it. It is not surprising that the butchers' name for the lungs of animals is 'lights', is it? The cardboard tube out of the plastic bag is where a bronchus would be in a real lung; you know what the disease is called when the inside of this tube gets infected.

127. How can worms breathe?

First of all, worms soak up air, especially oxygen, all over their skin. But where from, when they are underground? To find out about it, get a clear jar or beaker and fill it half full of earth (soil) from the garden, or from a flower-pot of soil. Run about the same amount of water into another jar or beaker of the same size (so also half full). Then quite quickly tip the water in on top of the soil. Watch what happens, on top and in the sides of the soil. Soil and water are both cheap, so you could do it a second time if you want to make sure that you see everything. Do the worms have anything to breathe down below?

Now, an important question for the worms—why do you think they come out of their holes and crawl about on the pavement and the playground in very rainy weather? Poor worms!

Note: when you clear up after this experiment, all the soil and water mixture should go on to the garden outside—*not* into the sink or toilet!

128. Fish need air—where is it?

Draw some water straight from the cold-water tap into a glass or clear plastic beaker, and stand it in the sun on a shelf or a window-sill. Leave it for an hour or two, and then look carefully at the sides of the beaker under water. You may see some small bubbles, which must have come out of the water.

Now draw some more cold water into the smallest saucepan you can find—or you can use a clean, empty tin. Stand the saucepan or tin very carefully on two bricks (real ones, not wooden or plastic blocks) and put a lighted nightlight under it, to heat the water. Look carefully every minute or so, without touching anything. Do you see any bubbles in the water? Are there any bubbles before it is hot enough to boil? If so, they are air-bubbles. Bubbles like this come out of water in the kettle, long before it is hot enough for steam. As the air bubbles burst, they make a small noise, and people say the kettle is 'singing'.

129. Air into water for the fish

Have you got a fish-tank with fish in it? Your own, or one at school? If so, there may be a 'bubbler' in it. This will be a tube going down into the water, with a little electric pump beside the tank pumping air into the water. At the bottom of the tank there may be a small block of hard stuff with many small holes in it, so that the air comes out in very small bubbles. An ordinary bicycle pump is no good for this, because the air bubbles must be very gentle as well as small, so that the stuff at the bottom of the tank does not get stirred up.

Think about ways to get many small air bubbles into the water—then try them. Blowing your own breath won't do for the fish-tank, because you will have taken some of the oxygen which the fish need. Will a cardboard-tube balloon pump, blowing down a few thin straws, do it? Or the same pump with a sponge pushed on to the bottom end of the tube from an old marker pen? The bicycle pump needs a valve, or water will come up as well as air going down. Test your ideas in a tank *without fish* to see which works best!

Burning and rusting

130. Candle under jar

This is an easy experiment to do, and it is easy to see what happens, but it is very difficult to know *why* it happens. Some books make it seem much easier than it really is.

All you need to start with is a short candle or a nightlight, a clean, dry glass jar, a plate and some way to light the candle. Use Blu-Tack to make the candle stand up firmly in the middle of the plate, light it, and put the jar upside-down over it. Watch. When you have seen all there is to see, take the jar off, fan some fresh air into it, light the candle again, and this time notice—with a sweep-hand clock or a digital watch giving seconds—how long the candle stays alight. Write down the time the flame lasted. It would be a good piece of science to do this two or three times.

Now get a smaller jar, but still big enough for the flame to be well away from the glass. Guess what will happen with the smaller jar, and test your guess. If you can get a bigger jar, try this too—guessing first and then testing. Your guess was almost sure to be right.

131. Three candles under three jars

Some people call this the 'Three Bears' experiment. You need three plates, three short candles or

nightlights (nightlights are good, because they can't tip over), and three clear jars: a big one, a middle-sized one, and a small one—but big enough to keep the glass away from the flame.

Stand the three candles on their plates in a row, light them, and then get three people to stand the jars upside-down over the candles, all at the same time. ('Ready, *go*'.) Don't say what you have guessed will happen, but watch carefully. This part is easy—the candles do what you thought they would do. (*Note*: don't stand the candles in water—it isn't needed, and it makes things more difficult to explain correctly.)

Now for a much harder test, and scientists are still arguing about why it does what it does. Get fresh air into the big jar, light its candle, and hold the jar over the burning candle flame, but not touching the plate. Hold the jar still, perhaps one or two centimetres up off the plate. Watch. When nothing more happens, check like a scientist by doing it again, and perhaps with the other candles and jars. That's an odd experiment, isn't it?

132. Fire brigade?

Firemen use water to put out fires. What does the water do? Think about this (there are at least two good guesses you can make), then try a mini-fire test. Collect a few wooden lolly-sticks, wash them and let them get really dry (on the radiator?). Now you need a big old plate or a big tin-lid, a short piece of candle or a nightlight, a pot with water in it, and matches or a lighter. Ask about using these.

Start your test by lighting the nightlight, and from it light one of the lolly-sticks at the tip. It is quite safe to hold the other end with your fingers—you can see when you have to drop it, and the plate or tin-lid is a safe thing to drop it on. Let one lolly-stick burn to about 1 cm of your fingers. Light the next one, and when it has burnt half-way along, dip the burning end in the water. Notice what happens. Can you light this stick again? Light one more dry stick, and dip it in water while it is still burning. Do the same things happen again as they did with the first one?

Did you see the red-hot bit of the stick while it was burning? What does the water do to that?

Drowning is stopping air for breathing, isn't it? Can the water stop air for burning too?

133. What makes things go rusty?

Take a good look at the oldest car which is parked near you. Talk to somebody with an old bike. You will find out quite a lot about things going rusty. Why don't people like it? Ask them, and think about it for yourself—perhaps it's *your* bike!

Try a small 'rusting experiment': you will need three of those ice-cream or delicatessen 'tubs' (about 15 cm cubes) with lids (just ask in the super-market) and all sorts of metal bits and pieces such as nails, screws, drinks cans, pull-rings, and so on. Also get hold of three small shiny 'tin cans' from something like baked beans. These will be part of a special experiment; make a few deep scratches in the tin on the outside of each of these three—say with a sharp screwdriver.

Now put something of everything in each 'tub'; put one on the radiator or window-sill—absolutely dry—and the second in the same kind of place, but with water in the bottom. Put the lids on, and look at the things every day. Did a car-owner say to you 'It's the salt they put on the roads in frosty weather that makes the car go rusty'? Well, try water *and salt* in the third tub.

What do the things in your three-tub experiment tell you? The first one had air in it, the second had air and water, the third had air, water and salt.

134. How can we stop things from going rusty?

First of all, look for some things which have gone rusty! Where have they been? You find a rusty nail or a rusty screwdriver, and somebody (you?) says 'I think it must have been left out -- --- ----'. Yes? Or somebody says 'Take your watch off before you go swimming, or the works will -- ----- '. So the first way to stop things from going rusty is obvious. But some things *have to* be out in the wind and the rain, such as bridges, and bicycles, and door-handles and drain-pipes. What can people do to stop them going rusty? Well, perhaps thay can paint things such as iron front gates, and railings, and railway bridges—and cars (a re-spray, with paint). What does the paint do? It keeps two things away from the iron, and so stops it from going rusty. And what can people do to keep gate hinges and clock works from rusting? They use something else, not paint, to keep water and air from the iron or steel.

Get some small nails of a kind which you know can go rusty. Put one or two in a cream-pot with water, one or two in another pot with oil on them, grease one or two with Vaseline (or lard) and, if you can, dip one or two more in a little house-paint. Cover them all loosely with a bit of wet newspaper—make it wet again every day for a week, and see which nails go rusty. Look out for rust everywhere—and see how to stop it!

135. Rusting needs water—does it need air?

This is a fairly easy question to test. You need a well-known kitchen and workshop substance called 'steel wool'. This is like Brillo pads without the pink soap, and it is used for the same kind of tough scouring jobs. It is good for this test because it goes rusty very easily.

Try it like this: get a glass jar (a clear, colourless instant-coffee jar is good if it doesn't have ridges

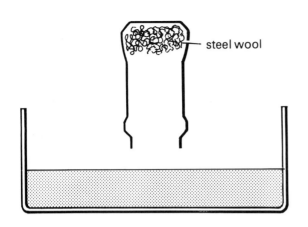
steel wool

in the glass at the bottom—because you need to be able to see clearly through it). Make a loose bundle of steel wool, and push it loosely to the bottom of the jar so that it fills the bottom. Prop it with a straw or a stick if it needs it. Then make it wet, and turn the jar upside down in a bowl (or ice-cream 'box') about one-third full of water. Tilt the jar to and fro until the level of the water inside and outside the jar is the same. Then leave the whole thing for a day, two days, three days—but look at it several times a day. What happens to the steel wool? What happens to the water level? What must have happened inside the jar? Does this give you an answer to the first question?

Water level and siphons

136. The top of water

A big, clear plastic lemonade bottle will be good for this. Fill it about half full of water, and put in some colour—a little powder-paint or some of the kind of food colour they use for birthday-cake icing. Stand the bottle on the table, and get down so that you can see straight across the top of the water. Would you say it looks 'flat on top'? This is the water surface.

Now think, before you do anything else—how will it look if you tip the bottle a bit sideways? Guess, and then try it. How would it look if you tilted it a bit more? Try it. And suppose you tilted it to the other side? Try it.

Now screw the cap on the bottle so that it won't leak, and let the bottle lie down on the table. Did you guess right about how the top of the water would look? And one more guess—how will it look if you turn the bottle right upside-down? Try it. Did you get all your guesses right? The top of water is *horizontal*, as you can see in sea pictures which show the horizon.

137. Marking the water level

Colour some water in a plastic jug, and pour it into a clear plastic lemonade bottle until the bottle is about half full. Stand the bottle on the table, and look across the top of the water. How can you mark on the bottle to show exactly how high the water comes? Can you make a mark with a crayon? Perhaps you can find a rubber band which will go over the top of the bottle and will stretch round the bottle to show just where the top of the water comes to. This would mark the top of the water—the water level—all the way round the bottle. Can you think of another way to mark where the top of the water is? Perhaps with sticky tape, or paper and sticky tape, or even an old lipstick? Find a good way to mark the water level. Then, just to see what happens, tip the bottle sideways a little. Does your mark still show where the water comes to? Now stand the bottle up straight again—is the mark right now? So you know what to do to get the water level marked right.

138. Watch water find its own level

This experiment looks like fun, but it can be used for scientific work too. Get two big funnels, the same size, and if possible the shape which has an upright edge round the funnel part. These hold more water than the ordinary ones. You also need some clear plastic tubing which will fit on to the stems of the funnels tightly—with no leaking.

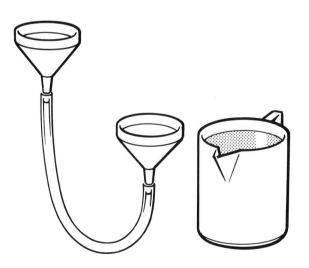

Push the funnels into the ends of the tubing. Now two people hold the funnels, while somebody else carefully pours water into one funnel. Do this slowly, and watch what is happening, and where. When only the tube is full of water, raise one funnel slowly, and watch. Then change over—lower the first funnel and raise the second, quite slowly. Watch again. Then put in a little more water, and try to get both funnels half full at the same time.

When you have made this happen, what do you know about the water level? Hold a ruler across, and see if you are right.

139. Water can run uphill in a tube

Water always seems to run downhill—of course. But there is one way to get water to run uphill, by itself, in a tube so that we can see it happening. The point is that the water is running *downhill* and

53

out of the tube at one end, and more water has to go in at the other end to take its place.

Try it like this: all you need is a length of clear plastic tube and two bowls or buckets. Stand one bowl or bucket on the table; this one has to be nearly full of water. Stand the second bowl or bucket (empty) on a chair beside the table. Now put one end of the tube down into the water, and—carefully—suck at the other end until the tube is just full of water. You do not need to drink any! Put a thumb over the end of the tube in your mouth, and without letting any water out (or any air in) put this end down into the bucket on the chair, and take your thumb away. Watch what happens.

What do you see at the bottom end? So what can you see at the top end? Drop a few used tea-leaves into the bucket on the table—they will show you the way the water is moving. Your tube is being a *siphon*. Take the bottom end of the the out of the bucket, and lift it up high. What happens? So you start all over again! Can you get this end of the tube exactly at the same level as the top of the water in the top bucket? Guess what may happen then. . .

140. Emptying the fish-tank

The water in the fish-tank needs to be changed sometimes. If the water looks thick, or the bottom is messy, it is probably better to change the water. But tipping up the tank is not the best way! So we use a length of plastic tubing as a siphon. One end of the tube goes down to the bottom of the tank, and the rest goes up over the edge of the tank and down into a bowl or bucket. But if you just put it like this, nothing happens. Try it. The tube has to be filled with water first—but better *not* by sucking at the end. Put the whole tube under water in a bowl, let it fill itself, and then keep your thumb over the end of the tube until it is under water again in the fish-tank.

Think out how to get mud out of the bottom without emptying the whole tank—and try your idea. Think out how to catch very small creatures which may get into the tube, or how to stop them from getting into it. . . Try your ideas.

Note: this *siphon* is different from the syphon which holds soda-water!

Water 'clinging' and the 'skin' effect

141. Is water sticky?

Try these tests and see what happens:

1. Get an old envelope and cut out the bit with the stamp on it. Make the bit of paper wet on the back to soak off the stamp. Wash all the gum off the back, wet the stamp and put it on the envelope somewhere else. Hold up the envelope—does the stamp stick? Pin it up on a board and let it get dry. Does the stamp stay on?

2. Wet two sheets of newspaper, hold them up by one corner, and let them touch one another all over. Can you hold up both sheets by holding only one by its corner? Try this with two more sheets of the same paper, dry. What does the result tell you?

3. Wet a piece of paper, any kind, any size, and flap it up against a smooth wall or the blackboard. What happens? Did you guess before you did it? And did you get it right? Leave the paper where it is—what will happen? Does it?

4. Get some small pieces of coloured paper, make them wet, and go round putting them up against all sorts of things—windows, cupboards, the door, other people's foreheads. . . (only not things like books or walls which will get spoilt by being wet). What do you find out from these tests?

142. Water holds things together

Look at yourself in the mirror when your hair is wet. If your hair is very wavy or curly, the effect won't show much, but if it is straight you may see hairs sticking together just because they are wet. Look at yourself again when your hair has got dry, and see the difference. You can try the same thing with a bit of fur or fur-fabric, or a soft paintbrush.

Find two plastic bags, and make one of them wet inside; then try to pull the two sides of each bag away from one another. Can you remember the feel of wet clothes against your legs in the rain? And how difficult it is to take off wet socks?

If your school has small plastic mirrors (from Osmiroid?), put two of them together, and see how easy it is to get them apart. Then put a drop of water between them, press them together gently, like a sandwich, and then pull them apart. How easy was it this time?

143. Water holds together across small holes

Try the question on other people: 'Will nylon tights hold water?'. You know what they are going to say, don't you! Well, try this experiment:

Get a jam-jar (the usual shape) and a piece of the nylon that tights are made of. You also need a rubber band which will fit tightly round the neck of the jar. Now, fill the jar with water; it does not have to be full to overflowing. Put the nylon over the top, fairly tightly, and the rubber band round to keep it covering the top of the jar.

Then, over a bowl or the sink, *just* in case, turn the jar upside down and hold it still, up in the air. There will probably be a few drops of water falling into the bowl—and then . . . nothing! If you tip the jar sideways it may 'leak' a bit, but try to hold it straight, upside down.

Of course, there are hundreds of tiny holes in the nylon, but the water holds on to the nylon and to the water on the other side of each hole—and if air can't get in, water doesn't come out!

144. What is waterproof? How waterproof?

What does it really mean when something is waterproof? Doesn't let *any* water through? Test some things you know will *hold* water, such as good plastic bags, and some things which may, or may not, stop water from coming through.

A good way to test materials (fabrics) is to fix a piece over the top of a clear jar (jam-jar?) with a rubber band round the neck, push the material in a little to make a dent in the top, and pour a small volume of water into the dent. Watch if anything comes through. You may have to wait some time, but you can leave this jar while you fit up another in the same way. Guess each time you test, and if you think the water has just soaked into the fabric, put some more on top. Some anorak material, for example, will probably keep rain out for a little while, until it is wet through—so it is not really waterproof!

Out of doors you could fit up model tents, using short garden canes and plastic bag or nylon over the top, and a watering-can to 'make it rain'. Some tents (real ones) will keep the rain out so long as you don't touch the fabric. You could test this too,

Can water come through an umbrella?

145. Water seems to have a skin on it

Steel is a heavy metal, and if you drop a steel screw into water it will go straight to the bottom. But sewing needles are made of steel too, and if you are careful you can make the thinnest ones float on water.

Fill a small bowl or a plate with water, then very gently put on top of the water a thin needle on a small strip of paper tissue. One layer is best, from a handkerchief or toilet tissue—and a piece only just big enough to take the needle.

Wait a little while, and the tissue will become completely soaked. Then *very* carefully push the tissue down into the water without touching the needle. The tissue will sink to the bottom, leaving the needle floating! Look across the top of the water—you can see that the needle is lying in a groove, a sort of 'dent' in the top of the water. There isn't any real skin there, but the top of the water holds up the needle as if there were one.

The insects called pond-skaters (or water striders) use this 'skin which isn't there' to hold them up on their six little feet on the top of a pond.

146. Drops and splashes

If you leave a tap dripping, you often find a lot of small drops of water on things in the sink, even if they were not under the tap. To find out more about how drops of water splash, you need something quite small out of which you can get water one drop at a time. The plastic lemon-shaped 'bottles' which are sold with lemon-juice in them will do very well for making drops of water, one at a time.

Now find a sheet of paper or card which goes darker when it gets wet, so that you can see where the drips and splashes hit it. Put this down flat, on the table or on the floor, and just let one drop fall on it from a height you can measure—say 25 centimetres up. See what the drop and the splashes do—if there are any splashes. Next, do the same thing from twice as high, with a different bit of paper or card underneath, so that the marks don't get mixed up. Try this from several heights, with a really high one as well. What difference do you find?

You could mark the drops and splashes with felt-tip pen dots, using a different colour for each height, and making a little table to show your code.

This test also works well on the playground, where wet marks look dark—until they dry up and disappear!

Water spreading in small spaces

147. Where water meets glass

Find a few glass bottles, tumblers, beakers and, if possible, a narrow glass tube closed at one end, like a chemistry test-tube. Now you need something you can pour out of, a very little water at a time. A good thing would be an indoor plant watering can!

First, fill all your glass jars, tumblers and so on about half full. Look very carefully at the edge of the top of the water—where it touches the glass. There is something odd about the edge of the water. Look at it from the side, with your eye at the same height as the water level. Make a big drawing of it, so that you could show somebody else what it looks like.

Now look especially at the top of the water in the narrow tube, or in the slimmest bottle you have found in your collection. You would think water would be flat on top, but is it? The special shape of the top of water in glass is called its *meniscus*. Other liquids have the same kind of shape too, but water shows it well. Look at the top of a cup of tea!

Now, just for fun, try to *over*fill one of your tumblers with the watering can. A drop or two at a time. . . Can you see how the water edge hangs on to the edge of the glass? Can you 'pile up' the water?

148. Floating table-tennis balls

Fill a clear tumbler or beaker about three-quarters full of water, and drop a table-tennis ball on top. Gently push the ball to the middle of the water surface, and let go. Can you make it stay in the middle? What does it do?

Now get some more water, and pour it carefully into the tumbler until it is really over-full, but none of the water runs over the edge. You can see that the top of the water bulges upwards at the edges—and this is important. What is the table-tennis ball doing now?

Carefully empty some water away, until the tumbler is about half-full. What does the ball do? Once more, fill the tumbler right up to the top; does the ball do what it did before?

The results you get in these two tests happen because of the way water 'holds on to' glass, and table-tennis balls! It is called *surface tension*.

149. Washing-up liquid and the 'skin' on water

Soap, and shampoo, and washing powder and washing-up liquid all have the same sort of effects on the 'skin' that water seems to have on the top of it. Here is an experiment which shows you one of the things that they do to it:

Get a large, clear beaker nearly full of water, and sprinkle ordinary talcum powder ('baby powder') all over the top. You only need very little. Now very carefully drop *one drop* of washing-up liquid on to the water right at one edge—and watch. Look at the top of the water, and look through the beaker into the water from the side. What is happening? What must the washing-up liquid have done, to make this happen?

You could try the same test with shampoo—or washing powder, though this works better if you mix the powder with a drop of water first.

Now see the effect another way: cut out a tiny boat-shape of paper, with a V cut into the stern (back end). Float it on water, and touch a tiny drop of washing-up liquid into the V. The 'skin' on the water will be stronger where there is no washing-up liquid; see what it does.
Note: you need really clean water each time; rinse

the beaker more than once between experiments, to get rid of the detergent (washing-up liquid, etc.).

150. Soaking up spilt water

If you are going to do experiments with water, it is a very good idea to cover the table-top with two or three big newspapers first. And if you spill some water on the floor, just flop two or three big news-papers down on top of that too. You can walk on the paper, and when you have finished you can roll up the damp paper and dump it in the waste bin.

How much water can newspaper soak up? Well, how much newspaper will you use for your test? You could start with one whole sheet, tear it in halves, then quarters and so on—the neat way would be to fold in halves, cut along the fold with a (not too sharp) table knife, then fold in halves again, cut again, until you have (64) pieces about 10 cm by 8 cm. Weigh all 64 pieces together; they will weigh about 20–25 grams.

Now, keeping the paper together in a little pack, either dip the lot into water, or hold it under the tap. Make sure that each sheet gets wet and then hold the bunch up by one corner to let it drain. This will not take long—just wait until it doesn't drip any more, but don't squeeze the water out. Weigh the damp paper. How much heavier is it now? Try this again with another newspaper! Is one better than the other at soaking up water?

Whichever paper you test, you can see why it does the job well if water gets spilt.

151. Bread, water and air

You need four pieces of bread for these tests, but they can be the four quarters of one slice. White bread works better than wholemeal (though it is not as good for you!). Look at the bread carefully before you do anything else; use a magnifier if you can. What does it look like?

Now leave piece **No. 1** flat on a saucer on the window-sill for the rest of the day, checking once or twice. Does it *do* anything? If so, can you guess why? Piece **No. 2** will help to explain; wrap it closely in clingfilm or a small plastic bag. This is what people do with sandwiches, isn't it? And when you look at No. 1 at the end of the day, you can see—and feel—why.

No. 3 goes into water, and stays there. Take it out again when you are looking at the others. Is this piece the same size now as before? How is it different?

Can you find out if there is any air in piece **No. 4**? What about squashing it flat? Can you? Or perhaps you could squeeze it in water; do you get any bubbles out? If you and a partner tried squashing another piece in water under a beaker of water, with your partner holding the beaker upside down over the bread while you squeeze it—you might even try to see if you could catch any bubbles of air coming out of the holes in the bread!

152. Water spreads through very small spaces

Paper tissues, kitchen paper towels, and paper table napkins (serviettes) are all good for mopping up water. To watch them at work, all you need is a quarter (square) of each, a few drops of left-over tea out of the teapot, or black coffee, and three dry saucers. Put each paper square on its saucer, drop a very little—two or three drops—of tea or coffee in the middle of the first one, and watch. Then do the same with the second, and the third.

You could test other kinds of paper too; look for the one in which the tea or coffee (really coloured water) spreads the fastest; this will be the best to use if you need to mop up a spill, won't it?

Water spreads upwards, downwards or sideways through very small spaces. We say it moves by *capillary action*, or *capillarity*. The Latin word for a hair is *capillus*, and the idea is that the spaces are as thin as hairs. They are often much narrower than hairs, but this is all to the good if we want to mop up water.

153. Water will climb through very small spaces

A good way to watch water climb is to get just a very little black coffee—a teaspoonful is enough—and one or two lumps of sugar. Hold a lump of sugar so that just one corner dips into the coffee; hold it still, and watch. Some people do this with doughnuts or biscuits—the same thing happens, but you cannot see it so well.

If you want to test the very small spaces in a lump of sugar, peel off a small patch on the side of an orange, push a lump of sugar half-way into the orange through the hole, and then suck at it! Of course, in the end the sugar will dissolve in the juice, but the test will have worked. If you haven't got an orange handy, try just sucking air through the sugar and you will probably feel that it works.

Now try the same sort of test as the first one, but this time with a piece of ordinary chalk, and some plain water. Choose half a stick of coloured chalk, a dark colour if you can, and stand it up on end in a little water, say in a saucer. Leave it to stand for a few minutes while you watch to see if anything happens. How do you know when, and where, coloured chalk is wet? Look at it again after about half an hour. What have you found out?

154. Can a little water run uphill?

If you have ever let the corner of your bath-towel dip into the bath-water, you know that the wet patch is bigger than the bit that went into the water. Try a few more comfortable experiments:

Colour some water, with ink or food colouring, or just use the last of the tea out of the cold teapot. Half-fill three or four clear beakers with this coloured water, put a pencil or ball-point across the top of the beaker, and hang a narrow strip of paper or cloth over each. You could use the edge of newspaper, a strip of old shirt, a narrow strip cut from a coffee-filter paper and another from a kitchen towel or a paper handkerchief. Let each strip dip into the coloured water. You will not have to wait very long for some results, but leave all the strips for about an hour, looking to see where the water has got to every ten minutes or so. In which strip does the water climb fastest? In which strip does the water climb furthest? Are there any strips in which the water does not climb?

You can make this an even better test if you use a tall jar, so that the water has a longer way to climb. Use plain water with coloured paper and fabrics in another experiment.

155. Watch water carry colours

When water creeps along in paper, it may be able to carry other things with it. If these things are colours, we can see what is happening. Try this:

You will need two or three felt-tip pens (not 'markers'), some blotting-paper or filter-coffee filter paper, dry cups or pots, and some way of getting *drops* of water just where you want them.

Make a small blob of colour (blue, brown or black will work well) in the middle of the flat filter paper (one thickness). Rest the paper flat on top of the cup or pot, and drip *one or two* drops of water on the spot of colour. Then watch. After a minute or two, put on another drop or two. Don't flood it!

You will find that the water spreads fast at first, but it goes on spreading slowly for quite a long time, and there are often very interesting results at the very edges of the damp patch.

Hang up your papers to dry on a line. While they are drying, try other colours, other spots in a pattern, straight lines, and so on. Try dripping the water at one side, and let it creep across. . . When the papers are dry, look carefully and see what colours of 'ink' were mixed to make the felt-tip pen colours.

156. Water carries colours upwards

Do you know somebody who makes filter coffee

for several people at once? If so, see if you can beg a few of the biggest-size coffee filters. You are going to use strips about 1 cm wide; work out how to get them as long as possible—from one thickness of filter paper. Then you need a few clean, dry jam-jars or clear plastic tumblers ('Glacier', from W. H. Smith's are good), two or three felt-tip pens in dark colours, and a few paper-clips.

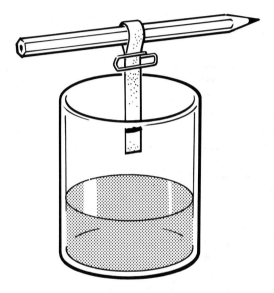

Cut strips of filter paper. Make a mark with felt tip across about 2 cm from the end of one strip; loop the other end over the felt-tip pen, fix it with a paper-clip, and rest the pen across the top of a tumbler or jar. The strip should hang down the middle of the tumbler, not touching the sides. Now carefully pour water into the tumbler, not wetting the strip, until the felt-tip pen mark is about 1 cm above the water level, but the bottom end of the strip is just under water. Leave it alone, and watch. You may find that the water carries some colours faster and further than others.

This method is used in many top chemistry labs to separate chemicals. This way of doing it is called *chromatography*.

Water and light

157. Water can be like a mirror

Get a clear tumbler of water. Really *look* at the top of the water. Look from the side, and from different angles. What can you see reflected? The window? The light? Hold your finger over the water—can you see it reflected? It is harder to see your own face, but try a puddle as a water-mirror. Look for reflections of clouds, buildings, trees and other people.

Now look for the water-mirror the fish see! Hold the tumbler up above your eye-level, and look at the underside of the top of the water. Can you see it looking silvery? Fish can see out of the water over their heads, but the rest is all 'water-mirror' for them. While you are looking from underneath, dip a pencil point into the middle of the water surface. Move it up and down, tilt it, take it out and put it back again. You can see how the shiny-looking under-surface of the water reflects like a mirror!

158. Looking for rainbow colours

You can get rainbow colours without any rain, but they aren't in the curved shape of the rainbow. The colours are called the *spectrum* colours—six of them, and always in the same order (indigo is really a dark blue, so six).

Stand a clean, empty fish-tank on a table in sunshine, and look all round it. Can you see any rainbow colours? Now fill it up with clean water, and look again. You may be lucky. Look at the corners, and look on the table and on the wall near the tank too. But you need bright sunshine—or perhaps you could use the bright light from the filmstrip projector shining in different directions. Look all the way round for spectrum colours.

There is another way to try for these colours using water. Fill a soup-plate or a shallow dish with water, and stand a mirror on one end in the water, sloping rather steeply. Make sure the mirror is in bright sunshine and tilt it more or less steeply, watching for rainbow colours. The water will split the sunlight up into the separate colours, and the mirror will reflect them back to you.

159. Send a beam of light through water

When you look at things through water, they often look strange. So try sending a beam of light through water and see what happens. You need a fish-tank or a clear plastic lunch-box with flat sides, and a bright torch or (much better) a slide/filmstrip projector. Why is this better?—just because it's much brighter.

Fill the tank or box with water, and put in something to show up the beam of light as it goes through the water. The best thing would be a drop or two of *red ink*, but if not, try *one or two drops* (not more) of homogenized milk! Stir. Now arrange to get the bright beam of light from your torch or the projector coming through a narrow, upright slit

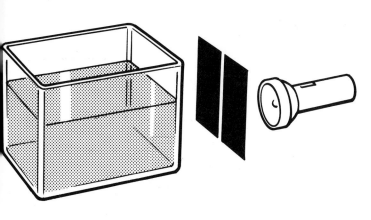

(like a cat's eye in bright light). You can stick two pieces of black card or paper across the front of the torch or projector, leaving a narrow space like a slit between them.

Make the room as dark as you can, and shine the beam of light into the side of the tank or box from a few centimetres away. Look at the angle at which the beam goes in and at the angle of the beam once it is in the water. Move the torch or projector, so that the beam goes in at a right angle to the side of the tank. Then move it so that the beam is hitting the tank at a 'sharp' or acute angle. What can you see? What does the water do to the beam of light?

160. How deep is the water?

People often say that water is deeper than it looks. How can you find out something about this? Maybe you could look at something in the bottom of the bath or, even better, because it is deeper, the bottom of the swimming baths. Look again as you get in—do your feet look as far away as they did when you were standing beside the water?

Now try the test with a ruler. Actually, you need two plastic rulers, both alike, and if at all possible get the kind which really start measuring from the *end*, without that little extra bit. The ones which

start at the end are called 'dead-length' rulers!

Put a fish-tank on the table, and fill it nearly full of water. Stand at one end of the tank, and hold one of your plastic rulers upright in the water with the end touching the bottom. Use it like a car dipstick, and see how deep the water is. Now hold the second ruler up beside the tank, and move the one in the water until the two rulers are close together, one in and one out of water. Move your head higher, then lower, and from side to side—looking at the lower halves of the two rulers from each position. Do they always look exactly the same, or can you find a place where one looks shorter than the other?

161. Looking at drops of water

Many taps drip. Find a tap which will drip, and look at the drops before they fall off. Try to make the tap drip so slowly that you can see the shapes of the drops while they are getting ready to fall off. Notice how the water seems to hold on to the edge of the tap until it is so heavy that it has to fall. You may find that the shape of the drop changes while you are watching; try to draw two drops, one when you first see it coming from the tap and before it is big enough to fall off, and then one which is just ready to drop.

People who draw pictures of rain coming down often draw the raindrops 'pear-shaped', with tails. When they draw somebody crying, they draw the tears this shape too. Drops from the dripping tap, and raindrops out in the open are *not* this shape—they are quite round—but this is hard to see because they fall so fast. (Photographs show what shape drops really are.)

But you can find out how the 'tear-drops' shape happens if you let the drips from the tap run down a sloping tray or a plate, one at a time. Try it. They seem to 'hang on to' the thing they are running down just as raindrops do on the window. Look at these too next time it rains. Perhaps this is where the artists got their idea for their drawings.

162. Looking at things through water

Looking at things through water sometimes makes them look very odd shapes. Try standing a pencil or a thin stick in a clear glass or plastic beaker half full of water. Hold it up so that you can look from the side, from near the bottom, from above the water level—from all angles. How many different ways does the water make your pencil look 'wrong'? Take it out of the water—is it really bent, or fatter at one end, or cut in halves? No? Put it back in the water again, and see if you can find any more strange effects.

Now try it with a ruler. Hold it straight up in the water and as close to your side of the beaker as you can. Then move the ruler slowly away from you to the far side of the beaker, looking at the part under water as you move it. What seems to happen? Move it towards you again to check.

All the 'odd' things you see, with your pencil or your ruler, happen because of the water, but if you saw the bit under water looking bigger (wider) than it really is, that would be partly because the water is in a round glass or beaker. You could use a clear plastic lunch-box or a fish-tank, half full of water, to check what happens if the water is in something with flat sides.

163. Looking through a bottle of water

Start with one of those large, clear, colourless plastic lemonade bottles—1½ or 2 litre size. Wash it out a few times, and let it dry if you have time. Hold it up and look through it at your fingers, and at a ruler against the side away from you—up and down and then across the bottle. Things don't look very different, do they?

Now fill the bottle with water, and screw the cap on tightly. Put your finger behind the bottle, against the side, and look through the bottle full of water. Do the same with the ruler, first one way and then the other. What do you see this time? When you hold the ruler across the back of the bottle, look first at the markings as they look through the water, and then—without moving the ruler—look at the same kind of markings beside the bottle (not through water). What is the difference?

Use your bottle of water to look at a bit of printed newspaper, an old stamp, a bit of a cloth, etc. What does the water in this shaped bottle really do?

164. A water magnifier?

Get hold of an ordinary glass or plastic magnifier—a lens. Check for yourself what shape it is, from the edges to the middle. Now try this:

You need a clear beaker, a piece of clear plastic bag or clingfilm, a rubber band which will fit the top of the beaker tightly, and some newspaper. If the beaker has a thin bottom (most plastic ones have), stand it on the newspaper. If it is a glass tumbler with a thick bottom, drop a small scrap of the printed part into the bottom.

Put clingfilm over the top of the beaker or tumbler and the rubber band round to hold it. With the tips of several fingers (say the three middle ones of each hand) gently press on the middle of the film until you have made a smooth curve down instead of the flat top. Carefully pour a little water into the clingfilm to fill it. Now look down through the water at the printing at the bottom. Compare the size of the printing as it looks beside the beaker and through the water. Compare the shape of your 'water magnifier' with the shape of the glass one.

165. Look in a drop of water

When it has just stopped raining, you can see drops of water hanging on twigs and the tips of leaves. There is somethimg odd about these drops—they look dark at the top and light at the bottom. Funny? As a scientist, you should try some tests on this. Get a drop of water to hang on something—a pencil will do—and test what you see. Move your hand up and down behind the drop to see what happens. Hold it between your eyes and a window—even better if there is a tree outside. See exactly what there is to see.

A drop of water is rather small. There is an extra-special way to find out more about it, if you can get hold of a *round* flask or bottle—a sphere. Look at things through it when it is 'empty' (full of air), and then again when it is full of water. This will be like a huge drop of water! Hold it up between the window and a piece of paper—if you move the upright piece of paper to the right place, you will get an extra-special result, and this will show you how the drops worked.

166. Bending water

You know about rubbing your pen on your sleeve and letting it pick up tiny pieces of paper—by static electricity. You know about stroking the cat on a warm sunny day, and getting sparks from its fur—that's static electricity—and you get the same kind of sparks from your own hair and your nylon clothes! And you know about rubbing a balloon full of air on your woolly and then letting it stick to the wall—that's still more static electricity. But somehow water doesn't seem to fit into this picture. Or does it?

Get a slow, thin stream of water running from the tap into the sink (or a bowl). Rub a ball-point pen (a Bic works well) on your sleeve or woolly, and hold it near the water as it runs down below the tap. Does anything happen? Try a plastic comb—rub it hard and then hold it near the stream of water. Some things work better than others—but that's static electricity again. . .

Water and air sounds

167. Water noises

This is an experiment for two or more people to do, because one person at a time is going to make the 'water noise', and the others are going to listen with their eyes shut! You need several things before you start, and these can be collected as a secret by one or two people, if you like. Good things to use would be a bucket, a big tin can, a 'soft' (expanded polystyrene) plastic coffee beaker, a blown-up balloon, a large, stiff sheet of cardboard, an empty shoebox, and a big empty saucepan. You can add plenty of other things as you think of them. You also need a big plastic jug of water, and something to catch the water in; the bucket may have to do this job.

Try two different ways of making different sounds with water:

1. A drop at a time on to different things—the tin, the coffee beaker, the balloon. . . what different sounds can you hear, with your eyes shut? 'Plink', 'plop', 'plup' and so on—try to catch each sound as exactly as you can. Then try to guess what the water is dripping on to, for each sound you hear.

2. Now listen to the different noises water makes when it is poured fast, in a stream from the jug. And you could try the 'gurgle' noises you get when you empty a big, plastic drinks bottle by turning it upside-down. What else helps to make the gurgle noises?

168. Water music, on a bottle glockenspiel (xylophone)

You need ten glass bottles, standing in a row—*not* hanging, that's too risky, as you know from the song. Use pint bottles, all the same shape.

Now, start with *two*. Put a little water in the bottom of one, and about three-quarters-fill the other one. Give each of them a double tap with a pen—'bing-bing, bong-bong'. Which makes the lower note? Pick them up, one in each hand. Which is the heavier? The bottles are all alike, so what makes the difference?

Next take two more bottles; leave one 'empty' and fill the other one right up. Guess how these will sound, then tap them and test your guess. Put them at the ends of the row—but which end for the low note? Think of a piano!

From here, go ahead and get the whole line of bottles with the right amount of water in each to make a musical scale. Where does the 'empty' bottle go? What have you worked out—the heavier the bottle of water, the . . . the note? Now play something on your bottle-glockenspiel/xylophone!

169. The voice of a balloon

When we speak or sing, the sound comes from our *vocal cords*, which are not cords at all, but are folds in the sides of our voice-boxes. The air we sing with comes up between these folds and makes them *vibrate* and the vibration makes the note.

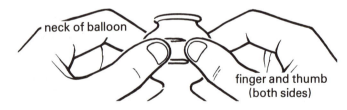

neck of balloon

finger and thumb (both sides)

You can get the same sort of thing to happen with an ordinary balloon. Before you blow it up, take hold of the two sides of the neck, just below the thick edge, with your two first fingers and thumbs. Pull sideways, stretching the rubber. The stretched bit is a model of 'vocal cords'.

Now blow up the balloon, not too tightly. Get hold of the two sides of the neck again, pulling it tight to keep the air in. To get the balloon to 'sing', carefully let the rubber neck where you are holding it go a little looser. Some of the air from inside the

balloon will get out, and you will be able to make different notes by pulling the rubber more tightly and less tightly. In our voice-boxes we do this with muscles which are much better at it, as you will hear.

170. Air and music

How many 'wind' instruments can you think of: recorders and tubas and mouth-organs and . . . They all need air to make them work—to make the music.

What do you know about the size of the musical instrument (especially its length) and the kind of note it makes? The descant recorder can play notes three octaves above middle C; these are very high notes. The tuba and the double bassoon can make notes about three octaves below middle C; these are very low notes. You can find out about these and other instruments in the Ladybird book called *Musical Instruments*, a very useful book.

Try this 'fun' experiment for yourself, and hear how the length changes the note of a 'wind' instrument. Get an ordinary waxed paper straw. Flatten one end, and cut off the flattened sides for about 1 cm, leaving two almost pointed pieces in the middle. Put this end into your mouth, in the space above your tongue but not touching it. Blow hard. At first you may not get anything, but if you go on trying you will probably get a loud squawk!

When you have got this going, snip off a bit of the straw with scissors, and blow again. Then snip off another bit, still squawking. What do you find out about the length of the straw and the note the air makes inside it? (Mind your nose when you snip!)

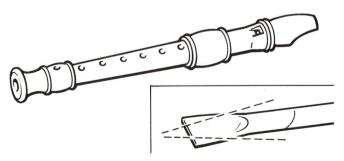

Notes on the sections

Light and heavy things; floating or sinking

The fact that a thing feels light or heavy is no true guide as to whether it will float or sink in water. The point to help children to see, from their own experiences—*not* by telling them—is whether the thing is/feels light or heavy *for its size*. A good way is to use two exactly similar objects, such as the full and 'empty' drinks cans. This makes the test a 'fair' one, which is a very important piece of scientific method—and completely understood by even the youngest children when this is pointed out.

Many floating objects contain air, from sponges to boats. They do not, however, float specifically because they have air inside them, but because the air makes them light for their size. The pupils who have tried the two drinks cans can think of an explanation in terms of 'Coke or no Coke' as an alternative.

'Things float higher in salt water' is at this stage an observation; density and relative density are later concepts, which need accurate measurement and calculation. Pictures from Israeli travel brochures, however, often supply very good photographs of people floating in the Dead Sea with heads, feet, hands and arms all above the water! This makes children begin to think about reasons; *don't* tell them too soon!

Displacement of air and water

The basic idea here, put very simply, is that two things cannot be in the same place at the same time. Children should not be told this—they should see it for themselves, perhaps through a number of different experiences. Part of the difficulty is that air is invisible—how can we know that it is there at all? Probably the best way is by seeing it 'esca-ping' in bubbles.

The displacement of water by something solid going into it is of vital importance for real comprehension of ideas such as floating, and relative density. Again, it is best grasped by having a number of small, simple experiences in which it can be seen to happen. When the basic fact is firm, and not until then, it can be taken further with displacement buckets, later displacement cans, and measurement.

Measuring and weighing water

This section includes three very important types of measurement: *volume* (or as children see it, size, or amount), *mass*—measured by balancing against given standard objects unfortunately called 'weights', and *weight*—the pull of gravity on the object being weighed, as measured by the stretching of a spring.

Children soon get used to the different quantities if they are introduced to them one at a time, with a chance to become familiar with one before the next is brought in. Clear 'definitions' are needed—for example, mass by balancing, weight by pulling. . . Unfortunately Osmiroid have introduced their 'Centicubes' as 'weights' for finding *mass*! Stick to 'Centicubes' as cubic centimetres—units of *volume* only—otherwise children will finish up trying to weigh in cubic centimetres. . .

The 'moon landings' are fading into history, which is a pity, because while they were in people's minds it was clear that the Americans were as big as ever on the moon, i.e. their masses were the same on the moon as on Earth, but their weights were only one-sixth because the force of gravity on the moon was that much smaller. 'Weightlessness', which children may ask about, and which is incorrectly illustrated in a *Science 5/13* book, happens when the pull of the Earth's gravity is neutralized in a spaceship, not using its rockets, which is then falling freely in space. There cannot possibly be a place between the Earth and the moon where there is no effect of gravity. Think of the millions of tonnes of sea water hauled up on our shores daily by the force of gravity of the moon causing our tides! The wind can affect the waves, but there is nothing else strong enough to make a high tide but the moon. It could not be the sun, as children may think out for themselves, because of the roughly one-hour-a-day difference in high-tide time.

Pupils may have to be told that *millilitres* for measuring volumes of liquids (i.e. water here) are 'the same size' as cubic centimetres. They can test this, of course. They also have to get used to the short forms: ml (millilitre); cm^3 or cu.cm. or c.c. (cubic centimetre)—all of which mean the same small volume of water (roughly 10 drops). This familiarization does not take children long, nor does it worry them if they have plenty of apparatus and plenty of time to use it.

Pupils used to pouring a litre of water from a tall measuring jar with *1000 ml* as the top marking and a coloured mark or a rubber band at that level into a 10 cm plastic cube will very quickly get the feeling that the 'shape' is not as misleading as shampoo and salad-dressing manufacturers hope it is for adults. Children quickly discover that 'tall' does not really mean 'more', though it may look like it.

Water pressure

The general idea of pressure in water—the deeper in the water, the more depth of water there is on top (of you, of anything) is grasped at once, especially if children can see parallel examples with, say, packets of sugar piled up on top of a hand on the table, or on a (protected and first flattened) piece of soft Plasticine or Blu-Tack.

In the playground they can check that the harder you squeeze a washing-up liquid bottle full of water, the further you can make it squirt, and so on. This helps to explain the water squirting out of the holes in the side of the plastic bottle.

Hot and cold water and air

At ordinary 'classroom' temperatures, the behaviour of both water and air is very simple: they both get bigger and 'lighter' as they get warmer. Similarly, they both get smaller, and therefore 'heavier', if they are cooled. Warm air rises in cooler air, warm water floats on cold water. Both of the simple 'thermometers' show the expansion which goes with warming, and the contraction which goes with cooling.

A classroom thermometer gives pupils a chance to read off the real temperature, but it is often more difficult to see the bulb. The coloured liquid in a bought thermometer is a kind of spirit (not 'meths' but rather like it). It can safely be used in snow and ice, but the liquid would almost boil if put in boiling water, and might well burst the tube.

Some printed schemes and books will tell you that a jar of air with a sheet of balloon rubber over the top is a 'barometer'. Don't be misled; certainly, a high atmospheric pressure will press a little more heavily on the rubber, and will compress the air inside the jar a little—*but* the difference which warming and cooling make is very much greater. Warm the jar a little, and it could suggest terrible storms!

Hestair Hope have recently (1983) introduced clear rigid acrylic tubing in 1 metre lengths (X2170/083) which would do very well for both models.

Water and air pressures

This section contains some very simple ideas, and some very difficult ones. The simplest is probably that air really does take up the space inside the containers usually called 'empty'. Following from this is the general idea, which children should also discover for themselves, that 'if the water can't get out, the air can't get in', and 'if the air can't get out, the water can't get in'.

The extremely difficult concept hinted at here is that of atmospheric pressure. The whole idea of the air above us pressing down, sideways and upwards, with a pressure of 15 lbs force on every square inch, or *1 kilogram force on every square centimetre* is so far from the evidence of our senses that to most people, not only children, it is literally unbelievable. However, something pushes the 'sucker' against the wall, and something pushes the milk up the straw. As there is nothing there to do it but air, so it has to be the air!

The idea of 'sucking' must be dealt with: we make a space inside our mouths, the air pushes the milk up into the space. A vacuum (should anyone mention it) is a completely empty space, and 'nothing' cannot suck, nor can it do anything else. The so-called 'vacuum cleaner' is a good resource in this area, because by starting with the back end and discovering that what it really does is to push air out at the back by a fan, it becomes logical that more air will go (be pushed) in at the front, quite incidentally taking the dust with it.

Several experiments described in other books are better avoided or left to secondary school physics. These include the 'collapsing can', which involves boiling water, understanding that the steam drives out the air in the can, then that the steam shrinks on cooling and finally that this produces reduced internal pressure which fails to stand up to the normal external pressure.

Other experiments are supposed to 'show that air has weight'. The real difficulty is that it has so little weight. If two flat balloons are balanced, and one is then blown up, the increased volume simply displaces more room air and, as with solids in water, this reduces its apparent weight almost to that of the other balloon. If two balloons are blown up, balanced, and the air from one is released, the 'jet' effect is likely to unbalance the whole apparatus. The only way to show simply that air has weight is to pump much more than the normal amount into a large, rigid container, such as a can with a bicycle-tyre valve soldered into a hole in the screw cap. The metalwork involved is more than most class teachers will want to tackle.

Bounce and bubbles

There is a lot of 'serious play' in this section. The activities on 'bounce' show that air can be compressed, but that it presses back—and in all directions (see the 'balloon-face' and balloon-in-beaker experiments). Experience with pumps emphasizes the 'springiness' of air—a very important (and historic) concept.

There is an enormous amount of science in 'soap' bubbles, but at this level the main points are purely observational, e.g. their lightness and their flexibility—flat underneath on water, flat sides when in contact with other bubbles, etc.

It is said that if you blow bubbles with warm breath out of doors on a very cold day, they will rise. Does this work? Try it. Under normal conditions, they fall slowly because of the weight of the soap solution, and there may be a drop underneath to demonstrate the reason.

The free bubble is a sphere because the air inside presses equally in all directions; blowing at a soap film in a ring (as provided with some bubble-mixture) shows the direction of the air during blowing.

The wind, spinners, parachutes, gliders

Though air is invisible, many of its effects are quite convincing. Most of the activities suggested have results which children can predict and then test in good scientific method. The specific work on gliders is organized to show how 'variables' can be tried out with as few external problems as possible. The use of telephone-book pages provides the standard material without cost (not using up your school stationery allowance), but at the same time allowing children full freedom to try one idea after another without constriction.

One or two small points: (a) children need help to distinguish between 'spinners' and helicopters—helicopters are powered, and just as able to go upwards as downwards, (b) ceiling tiles (expanded polystyrene/styrofoam squares) are a delight to children in this context—but they *are fragile*, and a lot of money can disappear rather quickly.

The ceiling-tile kites are so well worth making that it is a good idea to protect the edges with a strip of sticky tape along the underside before anything happens. What holds a kite up in the air? The air, of course, but the angle has to be right—roughly 45 degrees to the horizontal. The tail is essential, to hold the back end down. Several strips as streamers are better for ceiling tiles than the traditional single tail—simply because the string of one tail tears out.

Water in the air

There is a great deal of everyday observation in this section, but it is not often explained and therefore not often understood. The aim here is to help children to observe first and then to find out *how* each of their observations could have been caused. They can find out, for themselves.

The basic facts are that there is almost always some water, as invisible water vapour, in the air. This is where water goes to when it dries up. Warm air can hold much more water in vapour form than cold air can, so if warm damp air is cooled, the water vapour turns back into visible water droplets (as mist, or a 'misty' patch from breath).

Drying-up, or evaporation, is speeded up by moving the air—wind, or fanning—as well as by warming. Drying up, or evaporating, water needs some energy, and this energy is taken as heat—so when water dries up some heat goes with it, and the thing or person getting dried by the air also gets colder.

All of these results can be found out by children, without being told; they can link each experience with their everyday knowledge.

Ice and snow

Given the right weather at the right time, and a bit of help from someone with an available fridge, this offers a great deal of slightly unusual scientific experience. Probably the only tricky fact is that water, unlike almost every other substance, *expands* just before it freezes. (The molecules of water re-arrange themselves just before they make the crystal pattern seen in snow and hoar-frost, and the new pattern takes up more room. This explanation is not useful to most children.) The observations children can make show *what* happens, and very few adults will have noticed what the children will see.

Perhaps the staff in the school kitchen could help with the (quite small) space needed in the fridge? There are many everyday examples of the happenings in the activities described—from burst water-pipes and split flower-pots to the fact that because water expands on freezing it must get lighter, therefore icebergs float. . .

Mixing things with water

Much primary science can be learnt from ordinary kitchen materials, and only very small quantities of those. The things specially chosen for this part of the water activities—coffee (instant), sugar, salt, milk, flour, instant mashed potato—are well known; they are picked out so that the science can be observed, tested, and understood, without any questions about 'special chemicals' interfering. There is absolutely no need to bring in things such as copper sulphate, which is poisonous, and so far from children's lives that what it does is meaningless to this age-group. Now, sugar is different.

It is worth while looking round for the shop which sells coarse or preserving sugar. It has no apparent advantages for jam-making, but it gives children the best easy example of the shape of real natural crystals that they are likely to see. 'Loaf' sugar is only sliced out of large lumps of tiny crystals all stuck together, and the true crystal shape cannot be detected. Growing sugar crystals is difficult, one of the main reasons being that the solution often goes mouldy before the crystals have formed. Try several dishes (dark brown coffee-jar lids) of salt solution, and others of Epsom salts (still available if you try chemists' shops). Nobody can tell if one dish is going to give you good crystals or not, but two factors should be considered: the warm window-sill dries up the water quickly, and gives quick results, the cool shelf lets the water dry more slowly, but is more likely to provide bigger crystals.

Separating mixtures; things which will not mix

This section follows on very conveniently from the 'kitchen' materials of the previous activities. Ready-made filter-coffee filter papers are suggested instead of the traditional circles which have to be folded, and which may come unfolded.

Sawdust is an odd choice for early filtering practice, but it is often handy and is clean and easy to dispose of. Secondary-school textbooks tend to say 'sand'—but this almost always gets into the sink if juniors do their own clearing-up, which they should do, and the sand blocks the S-bend in the sink-drain. Caretakers also dislike sand being trodden into the floor. Sawdust is good here too!

The wax and oil experiences are already half-known, and are important in everyday life. The melted candle wax shrinks (contracts) as it cools, unlike ice in ice cubes and lollies, so the top of the cold drop of hardened wax is sunken in the middle. This is the normal pattern—ice is the (very) odd one out.

Plants and water

Of course children know that you have to put flowers in water to keep them fresh, so what they gain here is mainly 'experimental method'—checking and testing. The material suggested is 'weeds', so that the tests are as little destructive as possible. Perhaps it is a good idea to make sure that children know which are the weeds before they pick them? If the playground only has one tree, the alternative 'twig' is out, and children may have to go a little further afield for material.

Experiments which involve soaked peas could be followed by the usual planting-and-growing-peas projects. The more the material used can be seen to continue its useful life, the better; throwing things away tends to devalue them, and children will often suggest a follow-up activity. In this case it could be 'cooking them', naturally.

The dandelion-stalk experiment is just a bit of fun at this stage; the inside cells of a soft hollow stalk soak up extra water (by osmosis) and expand, while the outer skin cells stay the same size—so the strips of stalk curl up. The potato cells also take up water, and swell slightly, while those left to dry naturally shrink and go flabby. Good analogies are footballs and tyres—pumped up or soft (though with air instead of water).

Breathing

Many printed books and schemes are a little careless about the wording of some of these activities. For example, they ask 'How much air is there in your lungs?' Or they say 'Breathe out until your lungs are empty'. Both of these are obviously meaningless, since no child can flatten out its chest like a plastic bag. There is always a considerable volume of air left inside the chest, which is just as well!

Measuring the volume of air which can be breathed out is a standard experiment, but not too easy—chiefly because the large jar needed to catch the air must be full of water to start with, which makes it very heavy, and must be open top downwards in water, which is difficult to manipulate. A good motto for this particular enterprise is 'If in doubt, leave it out'. Blowing up a large plastic bag is a good alternative. The essential, though not obvious, fact needed to understand the breathing of fish (and crabs among other creatures) is that there is air *dissolved* in water and such creatures can get it out.

Burning and rusting

Burning is not an easy process for classroom work, so the activities are few and carefully chosen.

The candle under the jar turns up in almost every junior book or scheme, but it is wrongly explained in almost every one. Let us get it right: one-fifth of air is oxygen, *but* a burning candle never uses it all up. The candle goes out before it has used even *half* of the oxygen in the jar, so this test *cannot* show that 'one-fifth of the air is oxygen'. It is true that the bigger the jar the longer the candle will burn—but it is very interesting that the candle goes out even if the jar is well up off the table or plate, with plenty of room for more air to get in at the bottom!

The best thing is not to *tell* children anything about it until they have seen the results of several experiments—and then to tell them the truth, that scientists are still working on it, trying to find out the real explanation. Standing the jar in water makes it even harder to get the answer right, because what happens is that the flame heats the air, making it expand, and some air therefore gets out at the bottom. When the whole thing cools down again, water is pushed in by atmospheric pressure to fill up the space, and the rise in the water level happens because of heating and cooling as well as because of oxygen being used up.

Rusting needs water and air, but it does use up more of the oxygen in the jar, without the other problems.

Water level and siphons

Children only need a few practical experiences to see that water, in a bottle or a tube, settles itself so that the top surface is level—'flat across the top' as they themselves say. They need to see this happen in sloping bottles as well as in vertical ones, since older people without the practical experiences are sometimes able to draw liquid in a sloping test-tube as if it tilted with the tube! Pictures from travel agents' brochures, showing views of the sea where the sky and sea meet provide the vocabulary item 'horizon', and the 'ah-ha' reaction—'ah-ha, horizon, so horizontal!' i.e. 'flat across the top'. Able and observant children will see that this does not hold at the very edge of water in a jar or tube, where the water clings to the container, so turning the edge upwards. There are experiences dealing with this in the next section.

The peculiar case of the siphon is quite different. If the siphon tube is full of water, and the end in the air is lower than the level of water in which the other end of the tube is immersed, water will fall out of the open end—naturally. As the end in water is in water (!) more water is forced into the tube to keep it full. Atmospheric pressure forces it 'uphill' in just the same way as it forces milk into the straw, 'uphill' into our mouths. Children should find out as much about how the siphon functions as possible, e.g., the effect of raising and lowering levels, getting bubbles into the tube, etc., without being too bothered with explanations.

Water 'clinging' and the 'skin' effect

There are so many good observations to be made about the way water behaves that we can offer children activities of several kinds, without worrying about the advanced scientific explanations. Everyday language used accurately will not be 'wrong', but will help pupils to understand far more clearly than too early use of technical terms.

The 'skin' effect on the top of water is sometimes compared with the skin on custard; unfortunately this is not very useful, since on water there is no skin that could be lifted off. What really happens is that the water on top 'hangs together'. A better analogy would be to imagine a fairly large group of children in the playground facing outwards and trying to repel 'strangers' who attempt to get into the centre of the group from outside. Wherever the 'invader' tries to enter, there is a line of 'defenders', but the defenders change places with others of their own team inside the group so that there is no recognizable 'division of labour'.

Detergent weakens the 'skin effect', so that adding a drop at one side of a water surface means that the comparative 'pull' at the other side is stronger. The weakening effect also means that substances which were previously 'held out' now get in, or in the case of the talcum powder, fall through, and can be seen sinking to the bottom.

Water 'hangs together' under other circumstances, as for example when a drop is forming on a tap; it also 'clings' (adheres) to other substances, e.g., to the tap itself, to the side of a jar and to wet hair.

Water spreading in small spaces

It is precisely the fact that water clings to other substances (but not all—e.g., not to greasy ones) which makes water move through very small spaces, cracks and tubes. If the spaces, as in porous paper, are small enough, the pull of the water and the inside of the space on one another is strong enough to lift the tiny quantities of water against the pull of gravity. The force is obviously not enough to pull water up through wide tubes; in fact, the narrower the spaces (and therefore the lighter the amount of water inside), the higher the water rises. This shows well if clear pots of coarse and fine sand, both dry, are stood in very shallow water, with small holes in the bottoms of the pots. Children will sometimes know that plants in pots can be watered just by putting the water in the saucer—it can get up to the roots at the top too.

The separation of felt-tip pen inks which are carried up in porous paper is a source of much aesthetic pleasure as well as scientific curiosity. Who would have guessed what mixtures of colours are put together by the makers to get what looks like black, or dark brown. And the pathology departments of all large hospitals have thousands of pounds' worth of apparatus carrying out exactly this kind of process, identifying rare chemicals which could not be separated in any other way—so helping to diagnose diseases.

Water and light

The physics of what happens when light goes into and out of water becomes mathematical in the secondary school—but so often at that stage the actual experiences become 'demonstration experiments'. Primary children can make so many discoveries, without the theory or the long words, which will be of great value when they meet the 'laws of refraction' and so on when they are older.

In the same way, it is very helpful if children have seen the rainbow, or spectrum, colours produced by water in the corner of the fish-tank, so that they know that water can split light up into these colours. The detailed explanation of the formation of a true rainbow in the action of thousands of falling drops is quite difficult physics, but simple observations are a great help.

Probably very few people have ever understood, or even noticed, the special 'lens effect' of a drop of water hanging on a leaf in the sunshine after rain. The fact that it looks dark at the top and light at the bottom because it is acting as an inverting (convex) lens is an exciting discovery for anyone who is encouraged to look carefully, without being *told* either what might happen, or why. The scene behind the drop—tree, chimneys and all—is the more convincing when you see it for the first time for yourself, and upside down at that!

The spherical flask, bottle, or old-fashioned goldfish bowl, full of water, gives the same experience very much enlarged.

Water and air sounds

A good deal of the basic science of musical sounds can begin from a very few experiments. The bottle glockenspiel shows that the heavier the vibrating

L. I. H. E.
THE MARKLAND LIBRARY
STAND PARK RD., LIVERPOOL, L16 9JD

object, the lower the pitch of the note it gives; the balloon 'voice' starts off the whole topic of vibrations due to air—from which one can move on to the influence of the length of the air-column which vibrates in a wind instrument. Here are three starting points in three activities, and all three are linked. Children will tend to complain at first that they can't get a squawk from their straw. If the tip of the straw is not touching anything inside their mouths, it is almost certainly a question of a few more blows; persistence pays.

The 'water noises' activity is enormously enhanced if pupils can use a small portable tape-recorder.

Making different sounds, and identifying them, is good training in listening—and being silent with a conscious reason is new to some children. They can invent and develop thorough investigations, such as the effect of wind direction on audibility of sounds made at a distance, the (mathematical) effect of distance on loudness, and—if they can catch the right moment—the effect of approaching and retreating on the pitch of the police siren. They will also observe without noticing it that sound, being carried by air, travels round corners and obstacles in a way which nobody expects light to do. The field is open!

Useful apparatus

Apparatus to purchase as and when possible (sharing with the mathematics department?).

Hestair Hope (carriage free in Britain)
P1205 Litre set
X1789/000 Plastic measuring cylinder 1000 ml in ml
X1746/000 Polypropylene beaker 1000 ml
M0226/083 Osmiroid spring balance 1 kg
M2512/000 Set of 8 weights (masses)
X2170/083 Rigid plastic tubing 1 m
M1327/000 Aquarium

Osmiroid
Super Beamer balance 8410
8020 Primary rule 25 cm dead length (pk 10)
8635 Plastic tubing 4 m (or purchase from Boots' etc.)

E. J. Arnold
SM904 Plastic weights (masses) 2×(pk 50×1g)

From local shops: Blu-Tack, food colourings, straws, etc.

Key words

These words are relevant to the following units, and can be looked up in other books if needed:

absorption   115–121, 150–152
adhesion   141–143, 147
atmospheric pressure   46, 49–53, 66
buoyancy   1–3, 6–9, 11–23
capillarity   150–156
chromatography   154–156
cohesion   141–143
condensation   77–81
contraction   40, 44–46
density   1–8, 11–23, 32–35, 38, 39
displacement   8–26
evaporation   41, 59, 75, 76, 107, 108
expansion   40, 42–46, 96–98
freezing mixture   94, 95, 97
mass   32–35
osmosis   119, 120
respiration   122–129
solubility   99–106, 111–114
surface tension   141–149
transpiration   116
volume   24–30, 122–125
water cycle   76–81, 84, 108
weight   16, 17, 31

171703

This book is to be returned on or before
the last date stamped below.

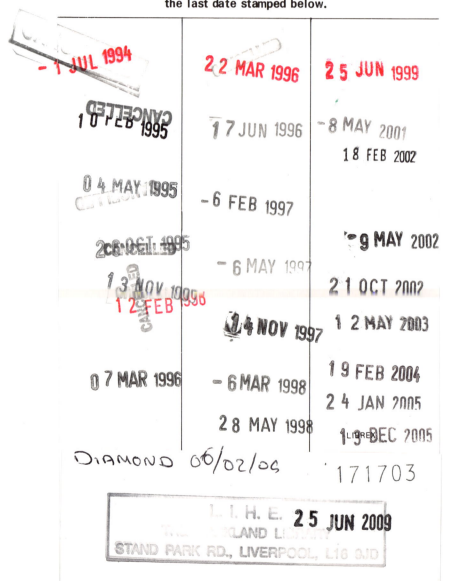

- 1 JUL 1994   2 2 MAR 1996   2 5 JUN 1999

CANCELLED
1 0 FEB 1995   1 7 JUN 1996   - 8 MAY 2001

18 FEB 2002

0 4 MAY 1995   - 6 FEB 1997

2 6 OCT 1995   - 6 MAY 1997   - 9 MAY 2002

1 3 NOV 1995   21 OCT 2002

1 2 FEB 1996   2 4 NOV 1997   1 2 MAY 2003

19 FEB 2004

0 7 MAR 1996   - 6 MAR 1998   2 4 JAN 2005

2 8 MAY 1998   1 5 DEC 2005

DIAMOND 06/02/06   171703

L.I.H.E. 2 5 JUN 2009
STAND PARK RD., LIVERPOOL, L16 9JD